Introduction

Learning how to write well is a lot like learning how to play tennis or other sports. You will never become good at tennis if you don't practice a lot. You will never learn how to play tennis well if you only think about playing it or if you read books about it. The only way you learn how to be a good tennis player is if you spend a lot of time actually playing tennis. Beginning tennis players first learn how to hit the ball across the net and then spend a lot of time practicing how to serve. Finally, they can play a game with other people, but they are always trying to improve their skills. Learning how to become a good writer follows the same principles. Being a good writer requires a lot of practice. You can't learn how to write well by only thinking about writing or reading about writing. You have to write!

The first edition of this book was published in 2001, and I am thrilled that so many teachers and students over the years have turned to this textbook to teach and learn English writing. The basic structure of the book in this new edition remains the same, but the topics have been updated to reflect the interests and needs of today's students. Like the first edition, *Simply Writing: Step-by-Step Guide to Good Writing— New Edition—* is designed to give you plenty of opportunity, not only to write in English but also to develop your listening and speaking skills. It is divided into three sections: Simply Useful, Simply Skillful, and Simply Successful. The first section introduces you to basic, everyday English writing. You will learn how to write a diary, how to fill out different kinds of forms, how to send e-mails and letters, and how to write about travel. Once you gain confidence by learning these easy, real-life writing skills, you will be ready to move on to the second part of the book: Simply Skillful. In this section, you will learn how to write descriptively, make comparisons, describe how to do something, and express an opinion. Each chapter in these two sections also includes an exercise that enables you to achieve a greater degree of accuracy in your English writing. The third section of the book introduces you to English academic writing, starting with the basic paragraph. You will learn how to write a topic sentence for a paragraph and how to provide supporting details for that topic sentence. The last two chapters of the book show you how to write a five-paragraph essay, which is the cornerstone of collegiate writing.

One important feature of this book is the appendix, which both you and your teacher will find useful. The first appendix offers some instructions and exercises on punctuation and capitalization. Appendix II shows what an assignment should look like before submitting it for a class. Appendix III gives a variety of salutations for emails and letters that differ in formality. Finally, Appendix IV is a list of a wide variety of possible writing topics students can choose from.

This book would not be possible without Takahiro Imakado, whose extraordinary editing skills and attention to details guided every step in creating this new edition. I was very lucky to have him as an editor, and the users of this book will certainly benefit from his contributions.

Finally, I have an important message for students. Becoming a good writer involves a lot of hard work and dedication. It's not an easy thing to do, but it's not an impossible task either. All you need to do is to say to yourself that you can become a successful English writer! If you practice hard enough, you will! All you have to do is work at it, step-by-step.

Good Luck!

Diane Hawley Nagatomo

Simply Writing *New Edition*

A Step-by-Step Guide to Good Writing

Diane Hawley Nagatomo

KINSEIDO

Kinseido Publishing Co., Ltd.

3-21 Kanda Jimbo-cho, Chiyoda-ku,
Tokyo 101-0051, Japan

First published 2024 by Kinseido Publishing Co., Ltd.

Design   Nampoosha Co., Ltd.
Illustrations   Yukiko Abe

Photos
p.68   © Meinzahn | Dreamstime.com
p.77   © Jill Meyer | Dreamstime.com

 音声ファイル無料ダウンロード

https://www.kinsei-do.co.jp/download/4206

この教科書で 🎧 DL 00 の表示がある箇所の音声は、上記 URL または QR コードにて
無料でダウンロードできます。自習用音声としてご活用ください。

▶ PC からのダウンロードをお勧めします。スマートフォンなどでダウンロードされる場合は、
　ダウンロード前に「解凍アプリ」をインストールしてください。

▶ URL は 検索ボックスではなくアドレスバー (URL 表示欄) に入力してください。

▶ お使いのネットワーク環境によってはダウンロードできない場合があります。

🔘 CD 00　左記の表示がある箇所の音声は、教室用 CD（Class Audio CD）に収録されています。

CONTENTS

Members of International Club of Yamanote University

(They will appear mainly in the conversations of the Try It Out section.)

Natsumi (Japan)

Loves travel and shopping. She has a brother who wants to become an actor.

Rin (Japan)

Loves meeting her friends. She is a little bit messy. She has a sister living in America.

Kaiji (Japan)

Loves city life. He wants to work for an American company and live abroad someday.

Akito (Japan)

Loves to explain things. He is funny and wants to become an English teacher.

Emily (Philippines)

Loves karaoke and nature. She thinks living in the countryside would be wonderful.

Olivia (Australia)

Loves studying literature and watching movies. She misses her grandma very much.

Michael (US)

Loves cooking. He is a big fan of Japanese anime and manga.

Rahul (India)

Loves reading. He always gives good advice, but he is not good at cooking.

PART ONE

Simply Useful

 DAILY LIVES
Describing Events

 DOCUMENTS
Filling Out Forms

 BASIC COMMUNICATION
Writing Messages

 TRAVEL
Describing Places

Chapter 1

DAILY LIVES
Describing Events

Warming Up

Read the following sentences, match each sentence with the topic, and write the topic down.

1. _____

Today seven people showed up for soccer practice. We played until it got dark, and then five of us went out for dinner. It was almost 10 o'clock by the time I got home.

2. _____

I wish my hometown wasn't so far away from Tokyo. I miss my family, and I want to see them. Too bad the train tickets are so expensive!

3. _____

Today was terrible! When I woke up, I had a sore throat and a fever, so I decided not to go to school.

4. _____

The teacher asked us to make group presentations next week. What should I do? I don't like speaking English in front of everyone.

5. _____

Emily wants to buy a new coat. She wants me to come with her to help her decide.

6. _____

Our flight left at 11 o'clock, so we had to arrive at the airport by nine. It was hard getting up early, but we were so excited. After all, it's our first trip abroad.

7. _____

I enjoyed myself last night even though it was a little expensive. The food was delicious, and everyone laughed a lot.

8. _____

I have wanted to work for a publishing company since I was a child. I wonder if my dream will come true.

Topics

a. A party   **b.** Feeling homesick   **c.** Catching a cold   **d.** Taking a trip
e. English class   **f.** Club activities   **g.** Going shopping   **h.** Dreams for the future

Getting Ready

Unscramble the words in parentheses in each sentence and choose the picture that matches it best. Capitalize the first word of your sentence if necessary.

( )

( )

( )

( )

( )

a. I met with Olivia in Shibuya today. First, (we / restaurant / at / a / had / Italian / lunch / small). Then we went shopping. Olivia bought a new pair of shoes. I didn't have any money, so I couldn't buy anything.

b. Today was the first day in a long time that I didn't have to go to school or to my part-time job. I decided to stay home and clean my room. After that, (YouTube / concert / watched / favorite / singer's / my / on / I). In the evening, I played online video games with my friends.

c. (us / the teacher / today / a test / in / class / gave). He said we would have to retake it next month if we failed. I'm so worried because I didn't study at all. I hope that I passed the test.

d. Today was terrible! I woke up with a sore throat and a high fever. I called my friend, and she advised me to stay home from school. (the day / went / the doctor / bed / the rest / stayed / for / in / of / to / and / I).

e. Tonight's party was so much fun. I didn't know all of the members of the International Club very well before, but now I think I'm on good terms with everyone. (soon / can / we / party / possible / another / as / have / hope / I / as).

Try It Out 1

There is a conversation and a diary entry on the next two pages. First, practice these conversations with your partner. Then read the diary and fill in the blanks. Use the past tense of the verbs from the list below. Some verbs are used more than once.

DL 02   CD 02

1

Michael: Hi Rin! What are you doing?

Rin: Hi Michael. I'm trying to do my homework. My teacher said we have to keep an English diary this semester. We have to write at least 100 words a day. I don't know what to write about. My life is so boring.

Michael: People write about their daily activities in diaries. I've been keeping one ever since I came to Japan because I don't want to forget my life as an exchange student.

Rin: I suppose I could write about the International Student's Association party we had last week.

Michael: Or you could write about your part-time job. Anything is okay!

Rin: I suppose so. But it'll be hard writing so much English every day!

Rin's diary

Today ¹_____ the first day of this semester. I ²_____ all of my classes, but my English teacher ³_____ us a difficult assignment. She ⁴_____ we have to write an English diary. I ⁵_____ my friend Michael about that, and he ⁶_____ me to write about my daily activities. That ⁷_____ good advice. It'll be hard writing so many sentences every day, but I'll do my best! I want to get a good grade. So, this morning I ⁸_____ up at seven and ⁹_____ the eight o'clock train for school. Then I ...

| advise | be | catch | enjoy | give | say | tell | wake |

10

2 DL 03 CD 03

Kaiji:	Hi Emily! How's everything?
Emily:	Not so good. I tripped on the stairs at the station this morning, and I hurt my foot.
Kaiji:	Oh no! Did you break it?
Emily:	I'm not sure. It hurts a lot.
Kaiji:	Maybe you should go to the hospital to get an x-ray.
Emily:	That's a good idea. I don't have any classes this afternoon.
Kaiji:	I hope it's nothing serious.
Emily:	Me, too. The International Club is going hiking next weekend, and I don't want to miss it.

Emily's diary

On my way to school this morning, I ¹_____ on some stairs in the station, and I ²_____ down. I ³_____ so embarrassed! I ⁴_____ to my class as usual, but I ⁵_____ trouble walking. I ⁶_____ Kaiji and he ⁷_____ me to go to the hospital to get an x-ray. I ⁸_____ to visit the hospital after class. Luckily, I ⁹_____ break my foot. The doctor ¹⁰_____ me some bandages and ¹¹_____ me to take it easy for a few days.

advise   be   call   decide   do not   fall   give   go   have   trip   tell

Listen to the conversations and circle the right answers to each question. Then read the following sentences carefully and fill in the blanks with the appropriate words.

1   🎧 DL 04   ⊙ CD 04

Q1. Why can't Akito go out with Olivia today?
    a. He's waiting for the pizza delivery.
    b. He already has a date.
    c. He has many things to do at home.

Q2. What's the first thing Akito is planning to do?
    a. Talk to people about New Zealand
    b. Clean his room
    c. Write a report about the furniture of New Zealand

Q3. What's the furniture company going to deliver this afternoon?
    a. A desk
    b. A bookshelf
    c. A bed

Akito's diary

Today was the first time in a long time that I didn't have to go to 1_____, so I did many things. First, I 2_____ my clothes and 3_____ my room. Then I had an 4_____ with some people from 5_____. We talked about our 6_____ on New Zealand. Olivia came over in the afternoon, and we 7_____ a couple of movies. We 8_____ to order pizza for 9_____, but we decided to go out for ramen instead.

2   🎧 DL 05   ⊙ CD 05

Q1. What did Natsumi and Rahul do tonight?
    a. They went to a movie and to dinner.
    b. They went to dinner and to karaoke.
    c. They went to a movie and to karaoke.

Q2. What kind of food did they eat tonight?

    a. Turkish

    b. Italian

    c. Chinese

Q3. Where will they go next week?

    a. To a movie

    b. To a Turkish restaurant

    c. To an Italian restaurant

Natsumi's diary

> I had fun with Rahul tonight. First, we went to see an ^{1}_____.
> It was a little scary but ^{2}_____. After the movie, we were hungry,
> so we had dinner ^{3}_____. The food was great and
> the price was ^{4}_____! We ate a huge pizza and had Italian ice cream for
> dessert. Next weekend, we'll eat ^{5}_____ at a restaurant near
> our ^{6}_____. I heard it's delicious, so I'm really looking forward to that.

Simply Writing *Past Tense*

When you write in a diary you are often writing about events that have already taken place and the verbs you use need to show that. Many verbs end in "ed" to show the past. Sometimes the word changes completely. Check your dictionary if necessary.

Read the following sentences and change the verbs to past tense.

1. Today when I wake up I feel so bad. My head aches and my throat is sore. I go to the doctor and stay home from school.

    _____

    _____

2. I have a date with my girlfriend tonight. We see a movie, and after that, we sing karaoke.

    _____

    _____

3. I play tennis all afternoon with my sister. We have a lot of fun.

_____

_____

4. Emily call me up this morning and ask me to go shopping with her. I meet her at the station at eleven thirty, and we spend all afternoon in Shinjuku.

_____

_____

5. Today's party isn't much fun. It costs 5,000 yen and the people who are at the party aren't very interesting. The food isn't good and some guys drink too much.

_____

_____

6. I have a quiz in my history class this morning. I read the textbook last night and review the notes I make in class, so I answer all the questions easily.

_____

_____

7. I go to three companies this morning to get information about working at them. It takes me three hours to finish everything.

_____

_____

8. Today I don't wake up on time, so I'm late for school. My teacher is mad at me because I'm always late.

_____

_____

9. Last weekend I go to a hot springs hotel with my friends. We take baths and eat a lot of delicious food. I spend a lot of money, but I have a very good time.

_____

_____

10. I'm very busy today at my part-time job. There are many customers, so I stay behind the cash register and take their money all day long.

_____

_____

Let's Write

1 Pretend you are Akito and this is your online calendar. Then write his diary describing what he did today.

9:00	English Class
11:00	History Class
1:30	Tennis with my circle
4:30	Part-time job
9:00	Karaoke with Emily and Kaiji
11:30	English homework

Akito's diary

----

2 Next write down six things you did yesterday. Then write your own diary.

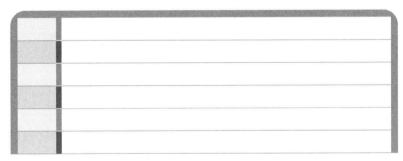

_____'s diary

Chapter 2

DOCUMENTS

Filling Out Forms

Warming Up

1 Read the following questions and match them with words and expressions that are commonly found on student visa application forms.

1. What's your educational background? _____

2. Where will you live in Australia? _____

3. What's your last name? _____

4. Where did you get your passport? _____

5. When's your birthday? _____

6. Where do you live now? _____

7. Where were you born? _____

8. Are you married or single? _____

9. When did you get this passport? _____

10. What's your first name? _____

11. What's your nationality? _____

12. When does your passport expire? _____

Words and Expressions

a. Family name   **b.** Given name   **c.** Date of birth
d. Nationality of passport holder   **e.** Date of issue   **f.** Date of expiry
g. Place of issue   **h.** Marital status   **i.** Residential address in Australia
j. Highest level of schooling   **k.** Present address   **l.** Country of origin

2 Read the following expressions and decide which kind of form the person is filling out.

1. _____	List work experience in the left-hand column.
2. _____	How long is your visit?
3. _____	What's your highest score on IELTS, TOEIC, etc.?
4. _____	Do you have a valid Japanese driver's license?
5. _____	Sign up to receive regular updates from our company.
6. _____	What's your opinion of our services?

Forms

a. Job application
c. Visa application
e. Newsletter subscription
b. International Driving Permit
d. Language school application
f. Customer feedback

Getting Ready

Unscramble the words in parenthesis in each sentence and match them with the appropriate forms. Be sure to capitalize the first word of your sentence. More than one choice is possible.

1. _____	(address / what's / shipping / your)?
2. _____	(visit / your / the / what's / purpose / of)?
3. _____	(personal / a / want / have / to / trainer / you / do)?
4. _____	(check-in / what's / date / your / of)?
5. _____	(any / have / skills / special / or / qualifications / do / you)?
6. _____	(picture / a / to / attach / forget / don't / recent) to the top of the application.
7. _____	(reasons / explain / for / please / your / here / studying).
8. _____	Please (all / you / list / attended / have / schools / the).
9. _____	(you / proficient / in / are / languages / what)?
10. _____	Please (employers / give / your / previous / names / the / of).

Forms

a. Online shopping form   **b.** Visa application   **c.** School application
d. Job application   **e.** Sports club membership application   **f.** Hotel reservation

Practice these conversations with your partner. Then read the paragraphs carefully and fill in the blanks with the missing words.

1 　　　　　　　　　　　　　　　　　　　　　　　　　　🎧 DL 06　💿 CD 06

Kaiji: I'm applying for an internship at an American company. I have to write an English résumé, but I'm not sure what to say.

Emily: First, at the top of the résumé, put your name, mailing address, telephone number, and email address. Then write your educational background with the dates you entered and graduated. Since you're still a university student, you write 'to present' instead of a graduation date. Then write down all your part-time jobs. That can show you're a hard worker.

Kaiji: All right. Anything else?

Emily: Be sure to mention any prizes, awards, or anything special you do. This helps the company know what type of person you are.

Kaiji: You mean like being the president of the International Club? And my volunteer work at an international kindergarten?

Emily: Exactly.

Kaiji's diary

Today I asked Emily how to write a résumé in English because I'm applying for an internship at an American company. It wasn't too difficult. First, I put my [1]_____ at the top of the résumé. Under that I wrote my [2]_____ address, [3]_____ number, and [4]_____ address. Then I added information about my [5]_____ background and [6]_____ experience. Emily said I should also include some personal information to show them what kind of person I am, so I wrote that I'm [7]_____, and I added my volunteer work at an international kindergarten.

2 🎧 DL 07 ⊙ CD 07

Natsumi: I made a questionnaire for my sociology class. Could you fill it out for me?

Michael: Sure. What's it about?

Natsumi: It's to find out about the types of jobs college students have.

Michael: How many responses do you need?

Natsumi: The teacher said we need to have between 10-20 participants in order to get enough data.

Michael: How many questions are there?

Natsumi: Just ten. It'll only take a few minutes to complete.

Michael: What if a student doesn't have a part-time job? How can they answer the questionnaire?

Natsumi: Oh, that's a good point! I'll add a question asking them to describe a job they'd like to have.

Michael: Good idea. Everyone could answer that, even if they don't have a part-time job now.

From Natsumi

Dear Friends,

Please take a few minutes to answer this ¹_____. It's for a school ²_____. I have to find out what kind of ³_____ Japanese college students have. I'd like to have ⁴_____ participants. There are just ⁵_____ questions. If you don't have a part-time job, just answer the last question. Thank you so much for your help! Natsumi.

QUESTIONNAIRE

Very often ☐

Often ☑

Sometimes ☐

Try It Out 2

Listen to the conversations and circle the right answers to each question. Then fill out the forms.

1

Q1. What kind of party are Rin and Rahul holding?
   a. Christmas party
   b. End-of-the-year party
   c. Going away party

Q2. Why do they need to make a reservation?
   a. The restaurant might get booked up.
   b. The vegetarian meals might run out.
   c. The date for the party is coming soon.

Q3. What information doesn't Rin want to receive?
   a. About the menu
   b. About future events
   c. About dating possibilities

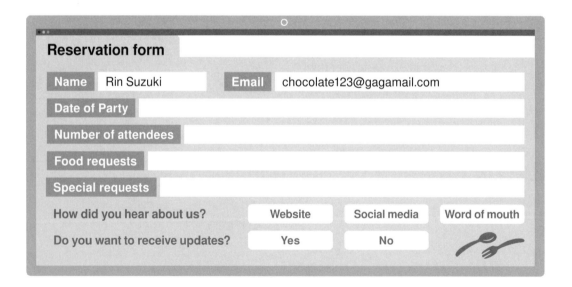

Reservation form	
Name Rin Suzuki	**Email** chocolate123@gagamail.com
Date of Party	
Number of attendees	
Food requests	
Special requests	
How did you hear about us? Website Social media Word of mouth	
Do you want to receive updates? Yes No	

2   🎧 DL 09   ⊙ CD 09

Q1. What job is Rin's sister, Honoka, applying for?
- **a.** Department store clerk
- **b.** Language teacher
- **c.** Sales representative

Q2. Where did Honoka graduate from college?
- **a.** UCLA
- **b.** Los Angeles City College
- **c.** Gambaru College of Business

Q3. What was Honoka's college major?
- **a.** Computer engineering
- **b.** Foreign languages
- **c.** Economics

Honoka's job application form

Name: _____

Address: 21 Baytown Road, Los Angeles, CA.

Age: 25

Position Applying for _____

Educational Background: _____

Major: _____

Work Experience: _____

_____

Special Skills: _____

_____

The first word of a sentence is always capitalized, and a sentence always ends with a period (.), an exclamation mark (!), or a question mark (?).

Complete sentences must have two parts. First you need to have a subject. That is a person, place, or thing. Then you need to have a predicate, which is the verb that says what the subject is doing.

Examples:

a. The boy jumps.

This sentence is OK because the subject is *boy* and the predicate is *jumps*.

b. is beautiful

This sentence is not OK because there is no subject. If we add a subject, it looks like this: *The weather is beautiful.*

1 Put a " ◯ " next to the words that make a complete sentence and an " ✕ " next to the words that are incomplete. Rewrite incomplete sentences to make them complete

1. _____ The people are very nice in Bali. _____

2. _____ swimming in the sea. _____

3. _____ The food. _____

4. _____ Linda visited some museums. _____

5. _____ hot and humid. _____

6. _____ I went by airplane. _____

7. _____ in Kyushu for a week. _____

8. _____ I took a tour of Hollywood. _____

9. _____ spicy, but delicious. _____

10. _____ I want to go again. _____

2 Read the following paragraph. Some of the sentences are incomplete. Rewrite the paragraph so that all of the sentences are complete.

Rin's diary

Last Sunday the weather beautiful. Didn't want to stay home and do homework, but I have to finish reading a book for my literature class. So, I a picnic lunch. I my book to the park to read there. I spread my mat under a tree and began to read. It very comfortable. Unfortunately, I fell asleep. I when it got cold. Began reading my book again after dinner.

Let's Write

1 Read Kaiji's résumé and then complete your résumé by adding your own information.

Kaiji's résumé

Name:	Kaiji Kobayashi
Mailing address:	3-21 Jimbo-cho, Chiyoda-ku, Tokyo, 〒 123-4567
Telephone number:	080-5555-1234
Email address:	K.Kobayashi@googlemail.com
Educational background:	Benkyo High School (April/2021—March/2024)
	Yamanote University (April/2024—present)
Work experience:	Oishi Ramen Shop (May/2023—September/2023)
	Super Convenience Store (December/2023—present)
Special Skills:	I got 650 points on the TOEIC test.
	I have a driver's license.
Personal information:	I'm president of the International Club.
	I do volunteer work at an international kindergarten.

Your résumé

Name:

Mailing address:

Telephone number:

Email address:

Educational background:

Work experience:

Special Skills:

Personal information:

2 This is the questionnaire that Natsumi wrote for her assignment. Answer it with complete sentences by using your own information.

1 Do you have a part time job? (If your answer is no, go directly to Question 10.)
   a. Yes   **b.** No

2 Where do you work?

_____

3 How many months have you worked at this job?

_____

4 How many hours a week do you work?

_____

5 How long is your commute from your house to your job?

_____

6 What do you spend most of your salary on?

_____

7 Do you plan to work in this field after graduation? Why or why not?

_____

8 Would you recommend the same job to your friends? Why or why not?

_____

9 How happy are you with your job?
   a. Very unhappy   **b.** Somewhat unhappy   **c.** Neither happy nor unhappy
   d. Somewhat happy   **e.** Very happy

10 Describe a part-time job you would like to have while you are a college student.

_____

_____

BASIC COMMUNICATION

Writing Messages

Warming Up

Read the following expressions and decide who the message is for. There could be more than one answer. Decide if the message is formal, informal or both.

1. Can you come to my party next week? _____ (formal / informal)

2. Thank you for the lovely present. I really love it.
_____ (formal / informal)

3. Thank you so much for your hospitality. I hope to visit you again someday.
_____ (formal / informal)

4. I'm very sorry, but I have to be absent from class today.
_____ (formal / informal)

5. Kyoto is a beautiful city! Check out these pictures.
_____ (formal / informal)

6. Could you please tell me if there is any homework this week?
_____ (formal / informal)

7. Congratulations on your marriage. I'm sure you'll be very happy.
_____ (formal / informal)

8. How's it going? Long time no see!
_____ (formal / informal)

9. I am writing to inquire about a position in the sales department of your company.
_____ (formal / informal)

10. May I visit your company next week to discuss our newest range of products?
_____ (formal / informal)

The message is for

a. a friend   **b.** a relative   **c.** a teacher or professor   **d.** a company

Getting Ready

Unscramble the words in parentheses in each sentence and choose the picture that matches it best. Be sure to capitalize the first word of your sentence.

1 (　)   **2** (　)   **3** (　)

4 (　)   **5** (　)

a. Are you free next Saturday? (concert / I / two / tickets / a / great / for / have).

b. (having / time / Hawaii / a / I'm / in / great!)! Check out my pictures! The weather is perfect, and the hotel is fantastic. Every day we go shopping and every night we eat in wonderful restaurants.

c. (last / dinner / thank / much / for / so / the / you / lovely / weekend). I had a great time meeting your family, and the food you prepared was delicious.

d. (away / grandmother / sorry / passed / hear / I'm / that / to / your / so). She was a wonderful woman, and I know how much you will miss her.

e. (would / inquire / company / in / a job / department / in / I / like / about / your / to / the / sales). I like meeting people, so being a salesperson for your company would suit me very well.

Try It Out 1

Practice these conversations with your partner. Then read the paragraphs carefully and fill in the blanks with the missing words.

DL 10 · CD 10

Emily: Do you want to go to karaoke next weekend?

Akito: I can't. I'm going back to my hometown.

Emily: But it's the middle of the semester.

Akito: I know, but I'll be doing teaching practice at my old junior high school. I plan to become an English teacher after graduation.

Emily: I bet you'll be a great teacher because you're always funny and good at explaining things.

Akito: I hope so. But I don't want to get behind in my classes. I need to email my teachers and let them know I'll be absent for a couple weeks.

Akito's email

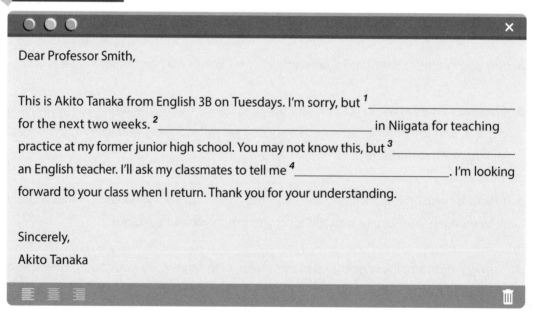

Dear Professor Smith,

This is Akito Tanaka from English 3B on Tuesdays. I'm sorry, but [1]_____ for the next two weeks. [2]_____ in Niigata for teaching practice at my former junior high school. You may not know this, but [3]_____ an English teacher. I'll ask my classmates to tell me [4]_____. I'm looking forward to your class when I return. Thank you for your understanding.

Sincerely,
Akito Tanaka

2

 DL 11 CD 11

Rin: Hi Rahul. I couldn't attend our sociology class last week because I caught a cold. Do you know if there's any homework?

Rahul: Sorry. I was absent, too. I overslept that morning. But I heard we have to write an essay about our hometowns.

Rin: Do you know the due date?

Rahul: Hmm. I don't know. Maybe next week?

Rin: What about the word count?

Rahul: Someone said it should be about 500 words. But I'm not sure if that's right.

Rin: I think I'll email the professor and ask her. If it's due this week, I want to get started on it right away.

Rahul: Can you let me know what she tells you?

Rin's email

Dear Professor Hopkins,

This is Rin Suzuki from your 10:40 a.m. class on Fridays. I'm very sorry, but
1 _____ because I caught a cold. I would like to ask
you about the 2 _____. I heard we have to write an essay about our
3 _____. Could you please tell me 4 _____ is due and
5 _____ is? Thank you so much.

Sincerely,
Rin Suzuki

Try It Out **2**

Listen to the conversations and circle the right answers to each question. Then read the following sentences carefully and fill in the blanks with any words that could fit logically.

1  DL 12 CD 12

Q1. What's Olivia writing?
    a. A postcard
    b. An invitation
    c. A letter

Q2. How often does Olivia write to her grandmother?
    a. Every day
    b. Every few weeks
    c. Every month

Q3. What's Michael going to do?
    a. Surprise his grandmother by visiting her
    b. Send a letter to his grandmother
    c. Buy some paper and an envelope

 From Olivia

Dear Grandma,

    How are you these days? I'm fine, and I'm still enjoying my life in Tokyo. Last weekend I visited ¹_____ with some friends from the ²_____. We didn't climb it, but we had a very nice view of it. It was a lot bigger than I expected. On the way home, we stopped at a ³_____ and ate seafood. It was delicious, but I really miss your cooking! Say hi to everyone for me.

Love,
Olivia

2  DL 13 CD 13

Q1. Why did Kaiji make this phone call?
 a. He was asking about a job opening.
 b. He wanted to make a complaint.
 c. He wanted to do telephone sales.

Q2. What kind of job does Kaiji have now?
 a. He works in a clothing store.
 b. He does telephone sales.
 c. He works part-time for a department store.

Q3. What does Ms. Smith want Kaiji to send to her?
 a. His résumé
 b. His interview schedule
 c. A copy of his graduation diploma

Kaiji's email

Dear Ms. Smith,

Thank you for speaking to me earlier today when I called to ask if you had any job openings for ¹_____. Attached to this email is ²_____. You can see I have had experience with ³_____ and I'm now working in ⁴_____. I enjoy serving customers. My long-term goal is to work in sales.

I can visit the A-to-Z Department Store for an ⁵_____ any time. Thank you very much for your time and consideration.

Sincerely yours,
Kaiji Kobayashi

Simply Writing *Future Tenses*

Will is to indicate a future action or a promise. Will is also used to volunteer to do something suddenly. **Be going to** is to express a plan or an action that is planned. In sentences you can often use both will or be going to. Will and be going to are followed by the base form of a verb.

Examples:

I will help you tomorrow.

I'll answer the phone.

I am going to go to the beach tomorrow.

I'm going to get a job in a bank.

The present tense and the present continuous tense can show a future action.

Examples:

My favorite singer's concert **is** next week.

The Yomiuri Giants **are playing** the day after tomorrow.

Fill in the blanks in the following paragraph. There may be more than one correct answer for some of the sentences.

I'm really looking forward to next weekend. After my last class on Friday, I'm
¹_____ straight home because my cousin ²_____ Tokyo. On Friday night we ³_____ at home, but on Saturday ⁴_____ early and go to Disneyland. This is her first time to go there, so she's very excited. We ⁵_____ until it closes, so I think we ⁶_____ very tired when we get home. On Sunday I'm ⁷_____ her to my campus. The International Club ⁸_____ a speech contest and she wants to watch it. I hope she has a good time in Tokyo.

Let's Write

Write an email to Professor Johnson to apologize for being absent and to ask about the homework. Some sentences should be in the past tense and some sentences should be in the future tense. Be sure to write "Dear Professor Johnson" at the beginning and "Sincerely," before you sign your name.

Chapter 4

TRAVEL
Describing Places

Warming Up

Read the following questions about travel and match them with the best answer.

1. What did you do during the vacation? _____

2. Who did you go with? _____

3. What did you do there? _____

4. What were the people like? _____

5. What was the weather like? _____

6. How did you go there? _____

7. How long did you stay there? _____

Answers

a. I went with three friends from my university chorus club.

b. Everyone was very nice. We got lost one day, and a kind person helped us.

c. Most of the time, it was great, but it was cool and cloudy for a few days because a typhoon was coming.

d. We were there for a week. The time passed so quickly.

e. I took a trip to Okinawa, and I had one of the best times of my life.

f. We visited beautiful beaches, ate delicious food, and went snorkeling.

g. We flew on XYZ Airlines from Haneda Airport. It was a very comfortable flight.

Getting Ready

Unscramble the words in parentheses in each sentence and choose the picture that matches it best. Be sure to capitalize the first word of your sentence.

1 ( )   **2** ( )   **3** ( )

4 ( )   **5** ( )

a. "Did you go anywhere during your summer vacation?"

"Yes, I went to Sydney, Australia, and (there / stayed / for / I / weeks / three)."

b. "Did you have a direct flight?"

"No, I didn't. A direct flight was more expensive, (six-hour / so / had / a / I / Singapore / in / layover). I was very tired when I arrived."

c. "What did you do there?"

"I climbed Sydney Harbor Bridge and I went to see a concert at Sydney Opera House. (saw / to / koalas / and / the / also / went / zoo / I)."

d. "What were the people like?"

"They were very nice and friendly. Whenever I had trouble, (was / always / someone / to / me / willing / help). People spoke slowly and clearly, so I could understand them."

e. "What was the weather like?"

"Well it was summer in Japan, so it was winter in Australia. (coat / it / a / so / cold, / had / I / wear / to / was)."

Practice these conversations with your partner. Then read the paragraphs carefully and fill in the blanks with the missing words.

1 　　　　　　　　　　　　　　　　　　　　　　🎧 DL 14 ⦿ CD 14

Rahul:	Did you go anywhere last weekend?
Olivia:	Yes, I went to Kyoto with someone from my seminar. We stayed with a friend from my hometown who's studying there. She took us to all of the famous temples and shrines.
Rahul:	What was your favorite place?
Olivia:	I guess it was Kiyomizudera. The street leading to the temple had many interesting shops and the view from the temple was gorgeous.
Rahul:	It sounds like you had a fantastic time.
Olivia:	We did. But we got tired from seeing so many places in such a short time.

Olivia's trip

Last weekend Olivia ^{1}_____ Kyoto with a friend from her seminar. They ^{2}_____ with Olivia's friend who took them to many temples and shrines. Her favorite place was Kiyomizudera because there were many ^{3}_____ nearby and the view from the temple was ^{4}_____. They had a ^{5}_____ time, but she said it was tiring to visit many places in just a few days.

2 　　　　　　　　　　　　　　　　　　　　　　🎧 DL 15 ⦿ CD 15

Emily:	Hi! I didn't see you at all last week. Did you go somewhere?
Kaiji:	Yeah, I went back to my hometown for a few days. It's in Kyushu.
Emily:	Kyushu? I saw there was a big typhoon in Kyushu last week. Were you there when it hit?
Kaiji:	Yes. It was terrible. It was very windy and rainy. We lost electricity for a few hours.
Emily:	Was your house okay?
Kaiji:	Yes, but all the flights were canceled, so I had to come back by train. It was so crowded that I had to stand the entire way. I was exhausted when I got back to my apartment.

Kaiji's trip

Kaiji made a short trip to Kyushu last week. Unfortunately, because of a typhoon, it ¹_____ heavily. The wind was so strong that all of the flights were ²_____.
He ³_____ back to Tokyo by train instead. Many people were on the train, so he ⁴_____ all the way. He was very tired when he got home that night.

Try It Out 2

Listen to the conversations and circle the right answers to each question. Then read the following sentences carefully and fill in the blanks with the appropriate words.

DL 16 CD 16

Q1. Where did Natsumi go?
   a. Italy
   b. France
   c. Indonesia

Q2. What did Natsumi do there?
   a. Learned French
   b. Visited museums and art galleries
   c. Ate delicious food

Q3. What was the weather like?
   a. Usually rainy
   b. Usually warm
   c. Usually hot

Natsumi's vacation

Natsumi went to ¹_____ for a month last year. She visited many
²_____ and ³_____ while she was there because
she had a lot of time. She bought ⁴_____ at the flea market
and she went to the countryside. She ⁵_____ by train because it was
⁶_____ traveling by car.

Q1. When did Emily go to Bali?
- **a.** Three years ago
- **b.** Two years ago
- **c.** One year ago

Q2. What did Emily do there?
- **a.** Play tennis
- **b.** Scuba dive
- **c.** Swim

Q3. What was the food like?
- **a.** Spicy
- **b.** Oily
- **c.** Sweet

Emily's vacation

Emily went to Bali [1]_____, and she had a wonderful vacation there. [2]_____ every day and enjoyed the beautiful beaches. The food was delicious even though it was a bit [3]_____. She hopes to go again someday because the people were very [4]_____ and [5]_____.

Simply Writing   *Prepositions*

A preposition is a word or a group of words that tells you where or when something is.
It shows time, direction, place, and location.

Study these prepositions and then fill in the blanks of Rin's diary.

Preposition	Places / Time	Example
in	city, country	I live **in** Tokyo.
on	street	My parents live **on** Ranch St.
at	your address	I live **at** 26 Daikyo-cho.
in	inside a place	I'll meet you **in** the bookstore.
at	a specific place	I'll see you **at** school.
in	month, year	I went to France **in** May.
on	day of the week, the date	I'll see you **on** Friday.
in	the general time of day, seasons	Let's go to the movies **in** the afternoon.
at	specific time of day	My class starts **at** two o'clock.

Rin's diary

I've always wanted to go to Australia, and last year my dream came true when I visited my friend [1]_____ Sydney [2]_____ August. John met me [3]_____ the airport early [4]_____ the morning [5]_____ August 15 and I stayed with his family for ten days. It was [6]_____ the middle of the winter there, so it was a little cold [7]_____ the early morning. [8]_____ noon the weather started getting warmer, so we went sightseeing [9]_____ the afternoon. His grandmother lives [10]_____ a small house just a block from the zoo, so I had lunch with her [11]_____ the day I went to see the koalas. In fact, she lives [12]_____ 200 Koala Way, which I thought was a wonderful address. John is planning to visit me [13]_____ Japan when he graduates from university. I'm looking forward to his visit. I want to show him all of the interesting things that we have here [14]_____ Japan.

Let's Write

Interview your partner about a trip they would like to take and write a short paragraph.

    a. Where would you like to go?

    b. How will you travel there?

    c. Why do you want to go?

    d. What will you do?

    e. What will you eat?

    f. Who do you want to travel with?

My partner wants to go to _____ someday.

_____

_____

_____

_____

_____

_____

_____

_____

PART TWO

Simply Skillful

Chapter 5

WHAT'S HE LIKE?

Describing People

Warming Up

1 With your partner, add phrases to A from B to make as many sentence combinations as possible and write down your sentences on a separate piece of paper.

A	B
• He's a short, thin man • She's slightly overweight • He's balding • She's tall • He's well-built • She's in her twenties • *Your idea*	with a mustache. and has a lot of wrinkles. with dark curly hair. with long black hair. and slim. and *your idea*.
• She's wearing a dark gray jacket • He has on a baseball cap • They're wearing jogging clothes • She's wearing a long black coat • They're wearing sleeveless T-shirts • *Your idea*	and a pair of jeans. and dark glasses. and a striped sweater. and a down jacket. and black high heels. and *your idea*.

2 Join these expressions together to make sentences. Use the correct pronouns and decide whether to use "and" or "but". "And" shows an additional idea and "but" shows an opposite idea.

• She's extremely kind,	(and/but) he/she's fun to be around.
• He's a little selfish sometimes,	(and/but) he/she always helps others.
• She's somewhat messy,	(and/but) he/she/everyone likes him/her.
• He's talkative,	(and/but) he/she makes everyone happy.
• She's always cheerful,	(and/but) he/she gets a lot done every day.
• He's lazy,	(and/but) he/she forgets to do his/her homework.
• She's energetic,	(and/but) he/she argues with others.

3 Match each occupation with the job description.

1. She's a doctor.	**a.** He grows rice.
2. They're teachers.	**b.** She's on the cover of many magazines.
3. He's a professional soccer player.	**c.** She works at a public library.
4. They're students.	**d.** He plays for Japan.
5. She's a librarian.	**e.** They major in economics.
6. He's a farmer.	**f.** They work for a computer company.
7. She's a model.	**g.** He directs love stories.
8. They're computer engineers.	**h.** He drives passengers around the city.
9. He's a movie director.	**i.** She works in a university hospital.
10. He's a bus driver.	**j.** They teach junior high school English.

Getting Ready

Unscramble the words in parentheses in each sentence and choose the picture that matches it best. Be sure to capitalize the first word of your sentence.

❶ (　　) ❷ (　　) ❸ (　　)

❹ (　　) ❺ (　　)

a. "What do you think of John?"
"I think he's handsome. (and / he's / slim / tall) and has dark curly hair. (cheerful / he's / outgoing / also / and). I like him a lot."

b. "I decided that (going / I'm / become / teacher / a / to)."
"That's a good idea. (and / you're / interesting / very / talkative). I'm sure the students will like you very much."

c. "What does your grandfather do?"
"He's a farmer. (he / potatoes / corn / grows / and). He's getting old now, but (very / still / and / he's / active / energetic)."

d. "What did the robber look like?"
"He was short and fat. He had long blond hair and was wearing glasses. (seemed / he / to / thirties / in / his / early / be)."

e. "(disorganized / your / messy / sister / and / is / so). Her desk looks terrible."
"I know, Mom, (reliable / but / is / organized / school / at / she / and). Everyone in her club counts on her because she's so responsible."

Try It Out 1

Practice these conversations with your partner. Then read the paragraphs carefully and fill in the blanks with the missing words.

1   🎧 DL 18   💿 CD 18

Olivia:	Guess what! I saw Tom Crocks last week at a restaurant in Ginza.
Michael:	You're kidding! Does he look the same as he does in the movies?
Olivia:	Yes, except he's shorter than I expected. And I think he wears a wig in the movies because he doesn't have much hair. But he's pretty tall and handsome with a muscular build. He was wearing a very expensive suit too. I thought he looked pretty sexy.
Michael:	Was he eating alone?
Olivia:	No, he was having dinner with Roberta Julian.

 Michael's letter to his grandmother #1

Olivia saw Tom Crocks having dinner last week with Roberta Julian in a Ginza restaurant. He was a little ¹_____ than she expected, but he had a ²_____. Olivia was surprised to see that he had little hair. In movies, he always has a lot more hair. Nevertheless, Olivia thought he was ³_____.

2   🎧 DL 19   💿 CD 19

(Continued from Conversation 1)

Michael:	What did Roberta Julian look like?
Olivia:	Well, she was as beautiful as she is in the movies. She had long curly brown hair and was tall and slim. She was wearing a simple pink cotton dress and white sandals.
Michael:	Oh, I wish I could've been there. Do you remember anything else about her?
Olivia:	Oh yeah. She was wearing a pair of glasses.
Michael:	Glasses? You're kidding!
Olivia:	No, I'm not. I was surprised because she never wears glasses in her movies. I guess she wears contact lenses when she's working.

Michael: Did you speak to them?

Olivia: No, but I wish I had said hello.

 Michael's letter to his grandmother #2

Olivia saw my favorite actress eating in a restaurant last week. She said she was as ¹_____ in person as she is in her movies. She wore a ²_____ and a ³_____. She also wore ⁴_____ while she was reading the menu. That surprised Olivia because she had never seen Roberta Julian wearing glasses. Then she realized that she probably wears ⁵_____ when she's working. Olivia wished she had been brave enough to say ⁶_____ to her.

Try It Out 2

Listen to the conversations and circle the right answers to each question. Then read the following sentences carefully and fill in the blanks with the appropriate words.

1   🎧 DL 20 💿 CD 20

Q1. What kind of cap was the thief wearing?
a. A blue knit cap
b. A green ski cap
c. A yellow baseball cap

Q2. What kind of clothes was the thief wearing?
a. A wool jacket and a pair of jeans
b. A raincoat and gray slacks
c. A red T-shirt and a pair of shorts

Q3. How old was the thief?
a. Mrs. Smith was sure he was in his twenties.
b. Mrs. Smith was sure he was in his thirties.
c. Mrs. Smith wasn't sure how old he was.

 **Police report**

According to Mrs. Smith, an eyewitness to yesterday's robbery, the thief was tall and wearing a ¹_____. He had on a ²_____

or [3]_____ jacket and a pair of [4]_____. He was possibly wearing [5]_____. He had a mustache and was wearing dark [6]_____. He was somewhere in his [7]_____ or [8]_____. If you see this person, please call the police immediately. He's a very dangerous criminal.

2

Q1. How old is Rahul's brother?
a. He's five.
b. He's twenty-one.
c. He's twenty-five.

Q2. What does Kamal look like?
a. He's of medium height and muscular.
b. He's short and has a slight build.
c. He's tall and skinny.

Q3. Which of the following is true?
a. Kamal is handsome and fashionable.
b. Kamal works at a gym.
c. Kamal invites the elderly to his home.

Rahul's Brother

Rahul has one brother in India. His name is Kamal and he's [1]_____ and [2]_____. He goes to the [3]_____ every day. He works in a department store, so he can buy clothes at a discount. In addition to this, he [4]_____ twice a week. He's a very nice person and everyone seems to love him.

Simply Writing *Sexist Language*

Writers need to learn how to avoid sexist language in their writing. Students used to be taught that masculine pronouns or nouns included both men and women. "Mankind" was considered to be both male and female humans. The names of many jobs were specifically for men. These days, however, people prefer to use *gender-neutral* words. That means that the words include both men and women. Take a look at the following.

OLD WORDS	NEW WORDS
chairman	chairperson, coordinator, head, chair
businessman / businessmen	businessperson / businesspeople
fireman	firefighter
mailman	letter carrier, mail carrier, postal worker
steward and stewardess	flight attendant
policeman and policewoman	police officer
ladies and gentlemen	people, everyone
mankind	humankind, people
man-made	synthetic, human-made, artificial

Simply Writing   *Dealing with Third Person Pronouns*

Pronouns are very important in English because they often determine the verb tense in a sentence. But when speaking about someone in general, like "a student," "a doctor," or "a teacher" it is difficult to decide whether or not that person is a "he" or a "she." To avoid this problem, it is better to say "students," "doctors," or "teachers," so the pronoun can be a gender-neutral "they."

OLD SENTENCES	NEW SENTENCES
Each student must submit his essay at the end of the semester.	Students must submit their essays at the end of the semester.
If a student is worried about his or her grades, he or she should ask the teacher for advice.	If students are worried about their grades they should ask the teacher for advice.
After a teacher grades a student's essay, she returns it to him or her.	After teachers grade students' essays, they return them to them.
A person who wants to buy a ticket should bring his money tomorrow.	People who want to buy a ticket should bring their money tomorrow.
Anyone who wants to apply for this job should submit his application immediately.	Anyone who wants to apply for this job should submit their application immediately.

Read the following sentences and rewrite them so that they are all gender neutral.

1. Today's scientific discovery was a huge step for mankind.

_____

2. OK, children. Anyone who wants to go on the picnic this afternoon has to clean his room first.

_____

3. This is a special discount for businessmen.

_____

4. Anyone who forgot his pencil needs to borrow one from his friend.

_____

5. That building was saved by firemen.

_____

6. The average college senior is worried about finding his job after graduation.

_____

7. Being a stewardess is a lot harder than you might imagine.

_____

8. This dress is made from man-made materials.

_____

9. If a student doesn't want to stay here, then he can go home.

_____

10. Mailmen are extremely busy at the end of the year delivering holiday mail.

_____

Let's Write

1 Write a short paragraph on a separate piece of paper describing a friend or family member.

2 Write a short paragraph on a separate piece of paper describing your favorite actor.

✔ Writing Checklist

☐ Is your name clearly written on the paper?
☐ Is your paper neatly handwritten or typed?
☐ Are all of the necessary words capitalized?
☐ Are all of the words spelled correctly?
☐ Did you use periods, commas, and other punctuation marks appropriately?
☐ Did you use the right verb tense for each sentence?
☐ Are all of your sentences complete sentences with a subject and a verb?

Chapter 6

WHAT'S THE DIFFERENCE?

Making Comparisons

Warming Up

The following chart shows how Japanese and American college students spend their time. Study the chart and then complete the sentences that follow.

	USA	Japan
Watching YouTube	35%	33%
Reading and/or posting on social media	70%	71%
Reading books	12%	15%
Eating dinner with family	25%	5%
Commuting to school	25%	90%
Playing video games	85%	85%
Shopping	10%	20%
Surfing the internet	80%	80%
Listening to music	35%	50%
Doing team sports	40%	60%
Doing individual sports (like jogging, yoga)	50%	45%

1. _____ students read more books than _____ students.

2. Many more _____ students commute to school than _____ students.

3. _____ students spend 20% of their time _____; whereas, only 10% of _____ students spend their time that way.

4. _____ American students and Japanese students spend equal time surfing the internet.

5. _____ students listen to music less than _____ students.

6. _____ students don't participate in team sports as much as _____ students.

7. The most popular leisure activity for both groups of students is _____ _____.

8. Only 5% of _____ students _____ with their _____.

9. The rate of reading and/or posting on social media is nearly the _____ for both groups.

10. Individual sports like yoga and jogging seem slightly _____ popular with _____ students than they are with _____ students.

Getting Ready

Unscramble the words in parentheses in each sentence and choose the picture that matches it best. Be sure to capitalize the first word of your sentence.

1 ( )

2 ( )

3 ( )

4 ( )

5 ( )

a. Emily is 164 cm tall. Olivia is 167 cm tall. (Olivia / a / Emily / than / is / taller / little).

b. I've been to France and Australia. Australia has a lot of beautiful nature, but (food / delicious / in / more / France / was / the).

c. Mount Fuji is the highest mountain in Japan. Mount Everest is the highest mountain in the world. (Mount Everest / not / as / Mount Fuji / as / high / is).

d. My mother and I are very similar. We both like to play tennis and go to karaoke. But (am / mother / is / a / than / tennis / I / player / better / my).

e. I like Japanese writers such as Haruki Murakami, Natsume Soseki, and Yoko Tawada. But (think / all / Murakami / writer / I / interesting / is / of / the / most).

Try It Out 1

Practice these conversations with your partner. Then read the paragraphs carefully and fill in the blanks with the missing words.

DL 22 ● CD 22

1

Natsumi:	Which dress do you think I should buy?
Emily:	I think both of them look very nice on you.
Natsumi:	Yes, but I can afford to buy only one.
Emily:	In that case, I think you should buy the dark blue one. You look better in that dress than the red one.
Natsumi:	Really?
Emily:	Yes. Blue suits you. It makes you look taller. Besides, it's much prettier than the red one.
Natsumi:	Oh, that's good! And it's cheaper than the red one, too.
Emily:	I know. That's another reason why I prefer it.

Emily's opinion

Emily thinks that although [1]_____ the red and blue dresses look very nice on Natsumi, she should buy the dark blue one because Natsumi looks [2]_____ in the blue dress. The color suits her very well. She also thinks it's a much [3]_____ dress. It makes Natsumi look [4]_____ than the red one does. And finally, it's less [5]_____ than the red one. That's a very important point for her.

DL 23 ● CD 23

2

Akito:	What do you think of our classes so far?
Olivia:	They're all pretty interesting, but my favorite is comparative literature.
Akito:	I agree. I think the teacher is really interesting. He's so funny. He's a lot funnier than the literature teacher we had last semester. I didn't like her so much.
Olivia:	You didn't like her because she was so hard. Everyone says she's the hardest teacher in the school.

Akito: That's for sure. I worked harder in that class than in any of my other classes. We had to read a lot and write so many essays. I'm glad it's over.

Olivia: Me, too. But there were some good points about that class.

Akito: Good points? I almost failed it.

Olivia: It's true that it was the most challenging class we've taken so far. But we learned a lot of things in it. It was a good experience to take that class.

Olivia and Akito's opinion

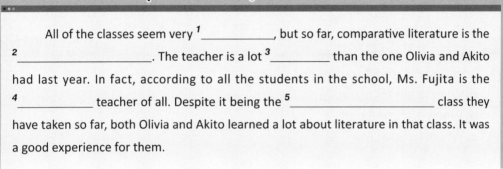

All of the classes seem very **1**_____, but so far, comparative literature is the **2**_____. The teacher is a lot **3**_____ than the one Olivia and Akito had last year. In fact, according to all the students in the school, Ms. Fujita is the **4**_____ teacher of all. Despite it being the **5**_____ class they have taken so far, both Olivia and Akito learned a lot about literature in that class. It was a good experience for them.

Try It Out 2

Listen to the conversations and circle the right answers to each question. Then read the following sentences carefully and fill in the blanks with the appropriate words.

 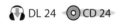

Q1. Who did Sophia ask for advice?
- **a.** Her father
- **b.** Her brother
- **c.** Her boyfriend

Q2. What's Sophia's problem?
- **a.** She has to move to New York.
- **b.** Her boyfriend doesn't love her.
- **c.** She can't decide who to marry.

Q3. Which characteristics describe Tyler?
- **a.** He's tall and rich.
- **b.** He has a good sense of humor and he's rich.
- **c.** He's good looking and fashionable.

Sophia's problem

Michael's sister, Sophia, has to make a difficult decision. She [1]_____ both of her boyfriends and can't [2]_____ which one to marry. Ryan is [3]_____ and more [4]_____ than Tyler. On the other hand, Tyler is [5]_____. He tells good stories and makes Sophia laugh a lot. In addition to that, Tyler is [6]_____ than Ryan. But the problem is that Tyler wants to [7]_____ to New York while Sophia wants to live near her family. Finally, Sophia isn't sure what she should do about her third boyfriend!

2   DL 25   CD 25

Q1. What are Rin and Rahul trying to decide?

    a. What to eat for dinner

    b. Where to hold a party

    c. Where to take a trip

Q2. Why doesn't Rin want to go to La Fiesta?

    a. She wanted to go somewhere quieter.

    b. She wanted to go somewhere cheaper.

    c. She wanted to eat a lot more food.

Q3. What kind of restaurant did Rin and Rahul decide on?

    a. French

    b. Mexican

    c. Italian

Rin and Rahul's plan

Rin and Rahul are planning a [1]_____ for the International Club. First, Rahul suggested going to La Fiesta, but Rin thought it was too [2]_____ there. She suggested The Parisian, but he wasn't [3]_____ if that was a good idea. He ate there once and said it was very [4]_____, and they gave very [5]_____ servings. They decided on Romano Pasta because the food is [6]_____ and it's much [7]_____ The Parisian. The interior is so [8]_____ that it makes diners feel like they're having dinner in [9]_____.

Simply Writing *Comparatives and Superlatives*

Comparatives: er - more

When comparing two things, use the '**er**' form (as in tall**er** and smart**er**) or '**more**' (as in **more** beautiful and **more** intelligent).

Use '**er**' with one-syllable adjectives and adverbs (tall, smart, and fast would become **taller**, **smarter**, and **faster**) and with two-syllable adjectives that end in '-y,' '-ple,' or '-ble' (happy, simple, and humble would become **happier**, **simpler**, and **humbler**). Note the spelling change with adjectives ending in 'y'.

Use '**more**' with adjectives with two or more syllables (useful, beautiful, and intelligent would become **more useful**, **more beautiful,** and **more intelligent**.) Use '**more**' with adverbs ending in '-ly' (quickly, happily, and surprisingly would become **more quickly**, **more happily**, and **more surprisingly**).

Superlatives: est - most

When comparing three or more things, use the '**est**' form (as in tall**est** and smart**est**) or '**most**' (as in **most** beautiful and **most** intelligent).

Use '**est**' with one-syllable adjectives and adverbs (tall, smart, and fast would become **tallest**, **smartest**, and **fastest**), and with two-syllable adjectives that end in '-y,' '-ple,' or '-ble' (happy, simple, and humble would become **happiest**, **simplest**, and **humblest**).

Use '**most**' with adjectives and adverbs that have two or more syllables (such as useful, beautiful, intelligent, etc.)

Note there are some exceptions with adjectives and adverbs.

Adjective/Adverb	Comparative	Superlative
good/well	better	best
bad/badly	worse	worst
little	less	least

1 Read the following sentences and choose the right form of the adjective or adverb.

1. I feel a lot (happier / more happy) now that I've finished my homework.
2. Why don't you sit in this chair? It's much (comfortable / more comfortable) than that one.
3. This is the (dirtiest / most dirty) room I've ever seen.
4. If you don't watch your money, you'll end up being the (poorest / most poor) person in town.
5. All my grades were bad, but the (baddest / worst) was for my English class.
6. I voted for that candidate because I think he's (honester / more honest) than the other one.
7. Why are you just sitting there doing nothing? You're (lazier / more lazy) than our cat!
8. My brother can run (more quickly / quicklier) than me.
9. That's the (deliciousest / most delicious) cake I've ever eaten.
10. She's the (smartest / more smart) of their three daughters.

2 Read the following sentences and fill in the blanks using the correct form of the words from the list below.

1. That dictator was one of the _____ in history. Many people died when he was in power.
2. I think that Brian Pott is the _____ actor today. All the girls love him.
3. My parents like my sister's new boyfriend because he always greets them. They say he's _____ than her old boyfriend, Ryan.
4. This is the _____ street I've ever driven down. I hope my car can fit!
5. Why did you get that problem wrong? It was a lot _____ than the other one.
6. Of all the children in the room, Nanaka is the _____. She never says anything.
7. If you think that you're _____ than me, why don't you solve the problem?
8. Even though Mrs. Jones has had a very hard life, she's still one of the _____ women in the neighborhood.
9. I think that the new assistant is _____ than the old one. She can complete twice as many things in half the time.
10. Stop eating all that candy! You're the _____ boy I know.

greedy	quiet	narrow	handsome	easy
efficient	polite	cruel	cheerful	clever

56

Let's Write

1 Write a short paragraph comparing yourself to one of your friends. Be sure to describe how you are similar and how you are different.

2 Write a short paragraph comparing college life to high school life.

✔ Writing Checklist

- ☐ Is your name clearly written on the paper?
- ☐ Is your paper neatly handwritten or typed?
- ☐ Are all of the necessary words capitalized?
- ☐ Are all of the words spelled correctly?
- ☐ Did you use periods, commas, and other punctuation marks appropriately?
- ☐ Did you use the right verb tense for each sentence?
- ☐ Are all of your sentences complete sentences with a subject and a verb?

Chapter 7

HOW DO YOU DO THAT?

Giving Instructions

Warming Up

1 The following sentences are step-by-step instructions on how to write a report for a class. Put the sentences in the right order.

1. First, _____

⬇

2. Second, _____

⬇

3. Next, _____

⬇

4. Then _____

⬇

5. Finally, _____

Instructions

    a. proofread your paper and make sure your name is on it.

    b. make rough notes on what you want to write about.

    c. write a first draft of your paper.

    d. gather information on that topic from the internet or the library.

    e. choose a topic that's interesting for you and that matches the assignment.

2 Read the following sentences on how to become a manga artist and put them in the correct order. Then match each sentence with its picture.

____ **a.** After you have your story, decide what your characters will say and put the characters and dialog into the panels.

____ **b.** Once your story is finished, share it with trusted friends so you can receive feedback. Revise your story if necessary.

____ **c.** The third thing that is important is to write an interesting story with a good plot that will keep readers turning the page.

____ **d.** Finally, send your completed work to a contest or magazine. You might become as famous as Hayao Miyazaki someday!

____ **e.** Second, a future manga artist needs to become familiar with the style of manga art, which includes putting pictures into panels.

____ **f.** If you want to be a manga artist, the first thing you need to do is improve your drawing skills through daily practice.

Getting Ready

Unscramble the words in parentheses in each sentence and choose the picture that matches it best. Be sure to capitalize the first word of your sentence.

1 (　) **2** (　) **3** (　) **4** (　) **5** (　)

a. Making curry rice is very easy. First, (bite-size / meat / onions / pieces / into / and / cut) and fry them in a pan with a little oil. Next, chop potatoes and carrots. Add them to the pan with water. After everything is cooked, add the curry roux.

b. Even though my apartment is a little far from the station (get / it's / easy / very / there / to). When you come out of the station turn left. There's a road that runs parallel to the railroad tracks. (that road / a / walk / down / store / until / straight / you / come / convenience / to). It should take you about 15 minutes. My apartment is right next to the convenience store.

c. Washing clothes is not difficult if you follow a few steps. (make / sure / first, / should / you) that you have nothing in your pockets. (your dark-colored clothes / second, / your light-colored clothes / separate / from). If you wash them together, the color of your clothes may change. Put the separated clothes in the washing machine, add soap, and then turn it on. (the clothes / after / washed / are), hang them out to dry.

d. Making a perfect boiled egg is very easy. Put the egg (cold / in / pan / a / water / of / and / on / the / stove / turn). As soon as the water starts to boil, turn off the stove. Put a lid (30 minutes / on / it / let / pan / and / the / sit / for). After that, peel the egg under cold water. It'll be delicious with salt.

e. Everyone should protect their computers from hackers. First, if possible, you should use a firewall. Next, make sure all of your software is up to date. (never / suspicious / links / unusual / open / emails / or), even if they look like they might have come from a friend. Finally, (passwords / choose / don't / anyone / carefully / with / them / and / share).

Try It Out

Practice these conversations with your partner. Then read the paragraphs carefully and fill in the blanks with the missing words.

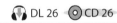

1	
Rahul:	Hi, Rin. What are you making?
Rin:	Curry and rice. Do you want to help?
Rahul:	I don't know how to cook.
Rin:	You don't know how to cook? Anyone can make curry and rice! I'll tell you how. First, you cut all of the ingredients into bite-size pieces. You need meat, onions, potatoes, and carrots. Then you fry the onions and the meat in a bit of oil. After the meat is brown, add the carrots and potatoes and fry them a little bit. Then add 750 ml of water and cook over low heat until the vegetables are soft.
Rahul:	That doesn't sound too difficult. Then what do I do?
Rin:	Add the curry roux to the pot and stir until the sauce becomes thick. See how easy it is? You pour it over hot rice and eat it.
Rahul:	So, how do you make rice?
Rin:	What?

Rin's kitchen

¹_____ curry and rice is very easy if you follow a few simple steps. ²_____, you ³_____ the meat and the vegetables into bite-size pieces. ⁴_____ you ⁵_____ the meat and the onions together until they're brown. ⁶_____, add potatoes and carrots with 750 ml of ⁷_____. ⁸_____ over low heat until they're soft. ⁹_____, add the curry roux, and ¹⁰_____ until the sauce becomes thick. It's delicious with hot rice.

🎧 DL 27 💿 CD 27

Olivia: Do you know how to go to Disneyland from Ikebukuro, Kaiji?

Kaiji: There're a couple of choices, but maybe the easiest way is to take the Yurakucho Line to Shin Kiba and get off at the last stop.

Olivia: How long does it take?

Kaiji: About half an hour.

Olivia: Then what do I do?

Kaiji: Then transfer to the Keiyo Line. If you get on the express train, it's one stop. Get off at Maihama Station. The entrance to Disneyland is a few minutes' walk away. You can't miss it. Just follow the crowds of people.

Olivia: So, it takes about an hour to get there from Ikebukuro. That's not so far at all.

How to get to Disneyland

It's easy ¹_____ to Disneyland from Ikebukuro. It only ²_____ about an hour. ³_____, get on the Yurakucho Line and go to Shin Kiba. That's the last stop. It should take about 30 minutes. ⁴_____ you need to ⁵_____ to the Keiyo Line. You can take either the ⁶_____ train or the ⁷_____ train. There will be many ⁸_____ at Disneyland, but I'm sure you'll have a great day there!

Try It Out 2

Listen to the conversations and circle the right answers to each question. Then read the following sentences carefully and fill in the blanks with the appropriate words.

🎧 DL 28 💿 CD 28

Q1. What's Michael doing now?

a. Eating cake

b. Drinking coffee

c. Having lunch

Q2. What are the ingredients?

a. Oatmeal and raisins

b. Nuts and dried fruit

c. Flour, sugar, cocoa

Q3. When will they eat the cake?

a. After it's baked

b. At school tomorrow

c. Next week

Michael's recipe

Michael is making a ^{1}_____. First, he mixed the ^{2}_____ ingredients together in a square baking dish. Next, he stirred in the ^{3}_____ ingredients. ^{4}_____ he sprinkled the top of the batter with chocolate chips. Now the cake is in the oven and it'll be ready to eat in ^{5}_____. He's going to bring the cake ^{6}_____ and share it with his ^{7}_____.

2

Q1. What does Akito ask Emily for advice about?

a. Weddings

b. Sightseeing

c. Packing

Q2. Why does Akito need to pack different kinds of clothes?

a. He wants to be fashionable.

b. He wants to do various things.

c. He doesn't want to wash his clothes while on vacation.

Q3. Where should Akito put the travel-sized toiletries?

a. Into the side pocket of the suitcase

b. Into his shoes

c. Into sealed plastic bags

Emily's advice

Packing for a short trip is easy if you follow these steps. First, [1]_____ what you want to take on your trip. Then lay everything out on your bed. Fold the biggest items like pants or jackets and put them neatly into the [2]_____ of the [3]_____. After that, [4]_____ smaller items like [5]_____ and shorts into balls and pack them into empty spaces. You can put [6]_____ and [7]_____ in shoes to save space. You don't want your clothes to get [8]_____, so put your shoes in [9]_____. Finally, pack your toiletries carefully so they won't leak into your clothing.

Simply Writing *Transition Words #1*

These are transition words that are useful when explaining a time relationship or the order of how something is done.

first	second	third	
afterward	finally	in conclusion*	meanwhile
previously	next	subsequently*	in sum

*mostly used for written English

Put the following sentences in the right order to make a paragraph. The first sentence is given for you. Underline all the transition words.

Living by myself is hard, but it has been a very good experience for me.

a. In conclusion, living alone isn't an easy thing to do, but it's a good way to learn how to become a responsible person.

b. Finally, I learned that cooking food at home is much cheaper than eating in a restaurant or buying prepared foods at a convenience store. When I started buying ingredients at the supermarket and cooking at home I was able to save a lot of money. I can use that money for my club activities or to buy new clothes.

c. Second, I found out that I have to be an organized housekeeper. When I didn't wash my clothes for two weeks, I didn't have any clean underwear. I had to buy a new pair so I could go to school that day.

d. First of all, I discovered that I must be responsible for myself. Since I live alone I have to make sure I wake up on time to go to school. If I oversleep I'll miss my classes and won't be able to pass them.

Let's Write

1 Your friend is planning to visit your house and you need to write down the directions. Explain how to get to your house from your school. Don't forget to use transition words.

First, you need to ......

2 What is your favorite thing to cook? Write down step by step how to make it. Don't forget to add transition words.

Name of dish: _____

Necessary ingredients:

1. First,

2.

3.

etc.

✔ Writing Checklist

- ☐ Is your name clearly written on the paper?
- ☐ Is your paper neatly handwritten or typed?
- ☐ Are all of the necessary words capitalized?
- ☐ Are all of the words spelled correctly?
- ☐ Did you use periods, commas, and other punctuation marks appropriately?
- ☐ Did you use the right verb tense for each sentence?
- ☐ Are all of your sentences complete sentences with a subject and a verb?

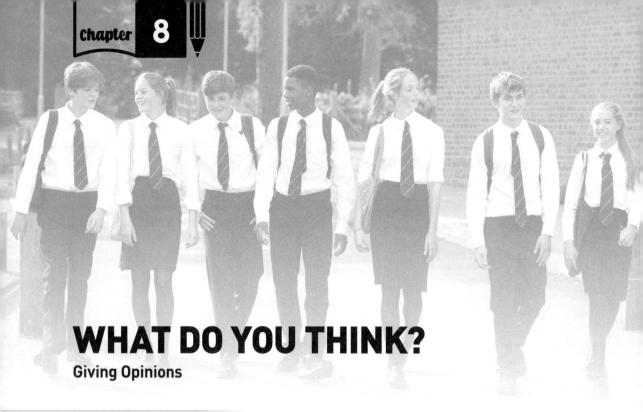

Chapter 8

WHAT DO YOU THINK?

Giving Opinions

Warming Up

Read the following questions and match them with the best answer.

> **1.** Which do you prefer, living in the city or living in the country? _____

> **2.** What's the greatest environmental problem today? _____

> **3.** What's your opinion of the two political candidates? _____

> **4.** Do you think children should be given smartphones? _____

> **5.** Should high schools eliminate school uniforms? _____

a. Well it's very clear to me that Sumiko Takahashi is the best person to do that job.

b. I'm sure many people would answer that living in the country is better, but I like all of the entertainment that city life can provide.

c. The world faces many problems, but I believe the greatest one that needs solving is climate change.

d. I think it depends on the age of the child. Very young children should not have smartphones. However, when they're around 11 or 12, such phones might be useful for them. Nonetheless, parents need to monitor the phones carefully.

e. In my opinion, students should be allowed to express their individuality in the clothes they wear.

Getting Ready

Unscramble the words in parentheses in each sentence and choose the picture that matches it best. Be sure to capitalize the first word of your sentence.

1 (　)

2 (　)

3 (　)

4 (　)

5 (　)

a. "Excuse me. I'm taking a survey right now. Which actor do you prefer, Brad Pitt or Tom Cruise?"
"Oh, that's a difficult question. (both / more / like / actors / I / they / good / are / , but / Brad Pitt). He has acted in some of my favorite movies."

b. "I'm thinking of moving to the countryside."
"Oh, I would never do that. (exciting / city / much / country / is / in / in / the / the / than / more / living / living)."

c. "Did you know it's almost impossible for underage people to go to a bar in the USA? You must show your driver's license to prove you're over 21 years old."
"Yes, I know. I totally disagree with that law because once a person graduates from high school, (to / they / able / should / want / decide / be / they / if / drink / to)."

d. "The government is considering adding a huge tax on cigarettes."
"Really? That's a great idea. (cigarettes / expensive, / might / become / if / people / start / not / smoking / very / young). That'll be better for their health."

e. "The other day, I read in a news site that many high school students refuse to attend school."
"I read that article, too. (education / terrible / it's / to / for / young / give / chance / up / good / for / their / people / those / a)."

Try It Out 1

Practice these conversations with your partner. Then read the paragraphs carefully and fill in the blanks with the missing words.

1

Natsumi: I don't know what to do about my little brother, Aki. He's decided to quit high school.

Rahul: That's terrible! High school is an important time in a young person's life. That's when you can learn many things that'll be useful later in life.

Natsumi: I know. He says he wants to become an actor and doesn't need to study subjects such as mathematics or English.

Rahul: That may be true to some extent, but a good education is never wasted. After all, if he learns English, he may be able to work in Hollywood.

Natsumi: Could you send him a message? I know he respects your opinion. He might listen to you more than to me or our parents.

Rahul's message

Dear Aki,

I'm ¹_____ your decision to quit high school. I know that you want ²_____ an actor and you ³_____ mathematics and English aren't necessary for your future. However, if you ⁴_____ English, you'll have a better chance of becoming a Hollywood ⁵_____! In my opinion, you should think carefully before you make a ⁶_____ that could change your life. You're only 17 years old. You have more than enough time to become an actor.

2   DL 31   CD 31

Olivia: I have to write an essay for my sociology class giving my opinion about the death penalty. I'm not sure what to write.

Akito: Well, how do you feel about the death penalty?

Olivia: I'm against it. I personally feel that the government does not have the right to kill someone. I also believe that there could be a mistake. What if someone was sentenced to death, but later it was discovered that person was innocent?

Akito: You have a good point. But I think the courts are very careful not to make mistakes. In my opinion, society is safer with the death penalty. I think crime would increase if the death penalty was abolished.

Olivia: I completely disagree. There are better ways to punish a criminal.

Olivia's essay

Some people may think that the death penalty is necessary because society is [1]_____ with it. They believe [2]_____ would increase if there was no death penalty. However, I [3]_____. I personally feel murder is murder. The government does not have the right to [4]_____. I'm also worried the court might [5]_____ and give the death penalty to an [6]_____ person. Therefore, in my opinion …

Try It Out 2

Listen to the conversations and circle the right answers to each question. Then read the following sentences carefully and fill in the blanks with the appropriate words.

DL 32　CD 32

1

Q1. Where are Kaiji's grandparents moving?
 a. To a foreign country
 b. To the countryside
 c. To another city

Q2. Why does Kaiji like city life?
 a. There are lots of people.
 b. It's easy to take walks.
 c. It's interesting.

Q3. How does Emily feel about nature?
 a. It's boring but quiet.
 b. It's never boring.
 c. It's not crowded.

Emily's diary

Kaiji's grandparents are planning on moving to the ¹_____ because they're tired of ²_____ life. He said they don't like dirty air and crowds of people everywhere. Kaiji is worried that they may become ³_____. Even though city life has a lot of interesting things such as good ⁴_____, and lots of ⁵_____ and ⁶_____, I think living in the countryside would be wonderful. My idea of a good time is ⁷_____ with birds singing around me.

2

DL 33   CD 33

Q1. What kind of movies does Olivia like?

a. Love stories

b. Action movies

c. Historical dramas

Q2. What kind of movies does Akito like?

a. Suspense movies

b. Love stories

c. Action movies

Q3. What do they decide to do?

a. Go to karaoke.

b. Watch both movies.

c. Stay home.

Olivia and Akito's likes and dislikes

Olivia has been looking forward to seeing *Death in Kanto*. She heard the
1_____ in the movie are really 2_____. But Akito thinks action movies
are nothing but 3_____ and 4_____. He wants to see his
favorite 5_____ in *True Love for Sightseers*. Unfortunately, Olivia thinks romance
movies are 6_____. They decided to go to 7_____ instead.

Use connecting words to write your opinion.

These connecting words help you give more information in your writing:

also   **besides**   **in addition**   **furthermore**   **both**

not only ... but also ~   **both ... and ~**

These connecting words help you give an example in your writing:

for example   **for instance**

These connecting words help you show a different idea in your writing:

however   **in contrast**   **on the other hand**   **instead**   **but**   **although**

Read the following sentences and fill in the right connecting words. Add capitalization if necessary.

1. Smoking is _____ harmful to a person's health, _____ it's bad for the environment.

2. A city provides more opportunities for employment than the countryside. _____, life is much more exciting there.

3. It's true that Taro Suzuki has more political experience than Kana Hashimoto. _____, Kana Hashimoto has the support of the general public.

4. Steven Spielberg has directed a number of serious films. *Schindler's List*, _____, is one of them.

5. _____ providing students with the opportunity to study a variety of subjects, general education classes give students a broader outlook on life.

6. _____ Charles Dickens and E.M. Forester are famous English writers, _____ I prefer Dickens because I like the characters in his novels.

7. That teacher is known as the hardest teacher in the school. _____, if you take that class you'll be sure to learn something useful.

8. My sister is a very tidy person. I, _____, tend to be messy.

9. My best friend is the kindest person I know. She's very friendly to the younger members of our club and helps them when they have trouble. _____, she's a volunteer at the foreign student center at her college. She does many things there; _____, she tutors the students in Japanese and helps them find part-time jobs.

10. I'll never go to that restaurant again. _____ it had a nice atmosphere, it was very expensive and too crowded. _____, the service was terrible. _____, the restrooms were dirty.

Let's Write

❶ Discuss with your partner the following questions. Be sure to use the words and expressions you have learned in this chapter.

  a. Which do you prefer, the city or the country?

  b. Cats make better pets than dogs. Do you agree or disagree?

  c. What's your favorite sport and why?

  d. Going to college is important. Do you agree or disagree?

  e. Smoking should be illegal. Do you agree or disagree?

❷ Choose one of the above topics and write a short paragraph stating your opinion.

✔ Writing Checklist

  ☐ Is your name clearly written on the paper?
  ☐ Is your paper neatly handwritten or typed?
  ☐ Are all of the necessary words capitalized?
  ☐ Are all of the words spelled correctly?
  ☐ Did you use periods, commas, and other punctuation marks appropriately?
  ☐ Did you use the right verb tense for each sentence?
  ☐ Are all of your sentences complete sentences with a subject and a verb?

Chapter 9

WHAT ARE THE FACTS?

Writing About Data and Facts

Warming Up

Some of the following sentences are facts and some are opinions. Put an "F" in front of each sentence that is a fact and an "O" in front of each sentence that is an opinion.

1. _____ Ming came to Japan in 2024 to study engineering.

2. _____ Ming must be very good at mathematics since he's an engineering student.

3. _____ Ming won a scholarship last year.

4. _____ International students are interesting to talk to.

5. _____ Kyoto University has an acceptance rate of 20-30%, making it competitive to enter.

6. _____ International students come to Japan to study because they can't get into good schools in their own countries.

7. _____ Seventy percent of international students who come to Japan study Japanese before they arrive.

8. _____ Teachers like having international students in their classes because they earn high grades.

9. _____ It's difficult for international students to make friends with Japanese students.

10. _____ More than 60% of international students interviewed stated that they had difficulty renting an apartment in Japan.

Getting Ready

Unscramble the words in parentheses in each sentence and choose the picture that matches it best. Be sure to capitalize the first word of your sentence.

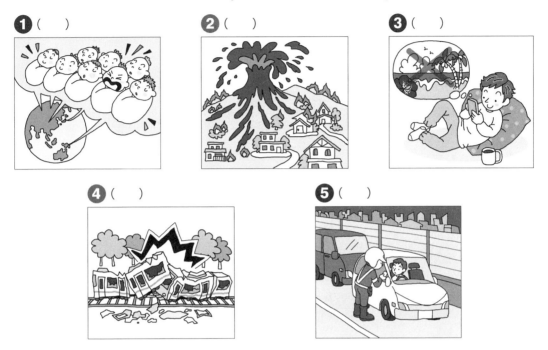

1 (   ) **2** (   ) **3** (   )

4 (   ) **5** (   )

a. (eyewitnesses / according / to), the train accident occurred at 12 noon.

b. (the / announced / report / that / news) the town near the erupting volcano had been evacuated.

c. (hundreds / police / of / say / people) have been arrested for drunk driving since they set up highway checkpoints.

d. (shown / recently / statistics / have / that) more people wish to stay home than travel during the holidays.

e. (recent / reported / a / online article / that) approximately 267 babies are born every minute in the world. That means the earth's population increases by about 215,000 people daily.

Try It Out 1

Laura Ingalls Wilder is the author of a series of books that are loved by children all over the world. Study this table describing Laura's life and answer the questions. Then fill in the blanks in the paragraph that follows.

Date	Laura's Age	Event
Timeline of Laura Ingalls Wilder		
1867	Birth	Born on February 7th, in the woods of Wisconsin
1873	six	Moves to Plum Creek
1878	eleven	Moves to Walnut Grove
1879	twelve	Moves to the shores of Silver Lake
1879	twelve	Laura's sister becomes blind
1880	thirteen	Experiences a terrible winter in De Smet, South Dakota
1882	fifteen	Gets a teachers' certificate
1883	sixteen	Starts teaching
1885	eighteen	Marries Almanzo Wilder
1886	nineteen	Gives birth to her daughter Rose
1911	forty-four	Writes her first article for the *Missouri Ruralist*
1932	sixty-five	Starts writing children's books
1932	sixty-five	Writes *Little House in the Big Woods*
1933	sixty-six	Writes *Farmer Boy*
1935	sixty-eight	Writes *Little House on the Prairie*
1937	seventy	Writes *On the Banks of Plum Creek*
1939	seventy-two	Writes *By the Shores of Silver Lake*
1940	seventy-three	Writes *The Long Winter*
1941	seventy-four	Writes *Little Town on the Prairie*
1943	seventy-six	Writes *These Happy Golden Years*
1957	ninety	Passes away

1. What happened in 1935?

2. What year was Laura Ingalls Wilder born?

3. How many books did she write in her lifetime?

4. How old was she when she wrote her first book?

5. What did she do when she was 18 years old?

6. What happened to Laura's sister?

7. What was Laura's daughter's name?

8. How old was Laura when she died?

Laura's life

Though she has been dead for many years, Laura Ingalls Wilder's books describing her childhood in the late 1800s are still read by children worldwide. She [1]_____ on [2]_____ and was the second oldest of four girls in her family. Her father wanted to live where there were no other people. He liked hunting and fishing in the wilderness. Because of this, Laura [3]_____ many times while growing up, and her books are set in the places she lived as a child.

Laura had a happy childhood, but a tragedy happened when she was [4]_____. Her sister Mary [5]_____ in [6]_____. Laura was an intelligent girl and wanted to become a teacher to earn money to send her sister Mary to school for the blind. When she was only [7]_____ years old, she got her teaching certificate and became [8]_____ in [9]_____. She didn't work for long because two years later she [10]_____. Rose, her daughter, [11]_____ in [12]_____.

Laura [13]_____ at the age of [14]_____ for a newspaper called the *Missouri Ruralist*. Her daughter, the writer Rose Wilder, encouraged her mother to write down the stories of her childhood. Rose believed children would want to know what life was like for children in the 1800s. Rose was right. Laura's first book, [15]_____, was published in [16]_____. It was hugely successful, and Laura became a well-known children's novelist in her [17]_____. She wrote [18]_____ more books before she [19]_____ at the age of [20]_____.

Try It Out 2

This pie chart describes how people manage stress. Study the chart and fill in the blanks. Then answer the questions.

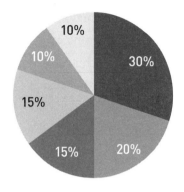

30%	Set personal goals
20%	Rely on planning, problem solving, and risk taking
15%	Look for ways to relax, such as mediation or reading
15%	Use little caffeine, alcohol or nicotine
10%	Exercise regularly
10%	Seek out people to spend time with

How people manage stress

Some people seem to handle stress better than others. We asked people who are successful at managing their stress to describe what techniques they used. First, [1]_____ of those interviewed said they set personal goals to work toward. In addition, 20% reported that they [2]_____. Fifteen percent of those interviewed said that they [3]_____ and [4]_____. An equal number of people (10%) said they [5]_____ and [6]_____. So, if you're having trouble dealing with stress, why don't you do what these people do and follow some of these useful techniques for a less stressful life?

1. Which stress lowering technique does the majority of those interviewed use?
2. What is the second most common technique for lowering stress?
3. Which technique do you believe to be the most important in lowering stress?
4. What do you do to lower your stress?

Simply Writing   *Subject Verb Agreement*

In English sentences, a singular noun needs to have the singular form of the verb, and a plural noun needs to have the plural form of the verb. Many students' writing errors are because their verbs are not in agreement with their nouns.

Examples: Singular

Incorrect   Only one of the children are late for school today.

Correct   Only one of the children is late for school today.

Examples: Plural

Incorrect   Many people who travel to Japan is tourists.

Correct   Many people who travel to Japan are tourists.

This kind of error can be avoided if you pay attention to the subject of your sentence.

Underline the subject and then choose the correct verb in the following sentences.

1. One of the students (is / are) going to turn in their homework late.

2. Do you think that four pizzas and one bottle of cola (is / are) enough?

3. The students at the restaurant next to the university (is / are) noisy.

4. Noriko is one of the women who (has / have) been to the Philippines.

5. This type of dictionary (is / are) very useful for students studying for that exam.

6. There (is / are) hundreds of fans at the baseball game, but my cousin is the biggest fan of all.

7. Some of the students in the English class (is / are) ready to do their presentations.

8. The cost of eating in restaurants (is / are) too high for most students.

9. Of all of the boys in the sixth grade, he (is / are) the only one who can't do that problem.

10. Everyone who cheered for that soccer team (was / were) pleased at its victory.

Let's Write

Interview five people on how they would spend ten thousand yen. Write the amount in the chart. Then write a short paragraph discussing the results.

	Person 1	Person 2	Person 3	Person 4	Person 5
New clothes					
Eating in restaurants					
Accessories					
Games					
Presents for friends/family					
Other					
Other					

_____

_____

_____

_____

_____

_____

_____

✔ Writing Checklist

- ☐ Is your name clearly written on the paper?
- ☐ Is your paper neatly handwritten or typed?
- ☐ Are all of the necessary words capitalized?
- ☐ Are all of the words spelled correctly?
- ☐ Did you use periods, commas, and other punctuation marks appropriately?
- ☐ Did you use the right verb tense for each sentence?
- ☐ Are all of your sentences complete sentences with a subject and a verb?

PART THREE

Simply Successful

Chapter 10

WHAT'S A PARAGRAPH? 1

Topic Sentences

Topic Sentences

What is an English paragraph? A paragraph is a group of sentences that discuss one idea. The main sentence in the paragraph is called **the topic sentence**. It is often at the beginning of the paragraph. The topic sentence has a *topic* and an *opinion* about the topic. The opinion is also called the **controlling idea** because it controls what will be said in the paragraph. Look at the topic sentence below.

My best friend Naomi is the busiest person I know.

The topic is "My best friend Naomi", and the opinion is "she is the busiest person I know". All the sentences that follow need to be related to the topic sentence.

Try It Out 1

1 **Read the sentences and put a " ○ " next to those that support the topic sentence and an " × " next to sentences that do not.**

> **Topic Sentence** My best friend Naomi is the busiest person I know.
>
> 1. _____ She wakes up early every morning to work at the convenience store next to the station.
> 2. _____ She has long black hair.
> 3. _____ She babysits her little brother every afternoon until her mother gets home from work.
> 4. _____ She goes to Korean conversation lessons several evenings a week.
> 5. _____ Most people like her because she's very friendly.
> 6. _____ Her mother is very busy too.
> 7. _____ She volunteers at an animal shelter once a week.
> 8. _____ Naomi's boyfriend works at a restaurant.
> 9. _____ She lives close to her grandparents.
> 10. _____ She's active in her circle.

2 Write a paragraph using the sentences that are related to the topic sentence.

My best friend Naomi is the busiest person I know. _____

_____

_____

_____

_____

_____

I'm certain that no one else I know is as busy as Naomi.

Try It Out 2

Put a " ○ " next to the sentences that can be topic sentences and an " × " next to the sentences that can't be topic sentences. Remember that a topic sentence needs both a topic and an opinion. On a separate piece of paper, rewrite the sentences that are not topic sentences.

> 1. _____ My dog is the smartest dog in the world.
> 2. _____ Watching television is a waste of time.
> 3. _____ The teacher scolded the students for one hour.
> 4. _____ My teacher is one of the hardest teachers in the school.
> 5. _____ Tokyo is the capital of Japan.
> 6. _____ The school is located in the middle of the city.
> 7. _____ Everyone should do sports for their health.
> 8. _____ The biggest problem in the world today is climate change.
> 9. _____ My friend lives far from school.
> 10. _____ That store sells a wide variety of goods.

1 The following sentences are about pets. Some of them talk about cats and some of them talk about dogs. Put a "C" next to the sentence if it says something about cats, and put a "D" if it says something about dogs. Underline the two topic sentences.

1. _____ I enjoy taking him for a walk every day because it helps me stay in shape.

2. _____ They're very quiet and won't disturb the neighbors by making a lot of noise.

3. _____ They never need to have their fur trimmed.

4. _____ They can spend a lot of time alone at home.

5. _____ My dog is a wonderful pet.

6. _____ You never have to give one a bath because it will clean itself every day.

7. _____ Cats are easy to take care of.

8. _____ He always sits next to me when I watch television and keeps me company.

9. _____ They don't need to be taken for walks every day because they can go outside by themselves.

10. _____ He wags his tail and gets very excited when he sees me.

2 Write two paragraphs about cats and dogs. Be sure to start with the topic sentence you chose above.

CATS

_____

_____

_____

_____

DOGS

_____

_____

_____

_____

Try It Out 4

1 Some of the following sentences talk about the *academic side* of university life and some talk about the *social side* of university life. Put an "A" next to the sentence if it says something about the academic side, and put an "S" if it says something about the social side. Underline the two topic sentences.

1. _____ I also made many friends at university after I joined the International Club.

2. _____ In my English class I have to read twenty pages a week.

3. _____ Not only have I become friends with students from my own university, but I have met a lot of people from different schools.

4. _____ University classes are a lot harder than those I took in high school.

5. _____ The teachers assign a lot more homework.

6. _____ I have some free time during the day so I can meet my friends in the student cafeteria for a chat.

7. _____ I have to write many reports.

8. _____ In addition, I have made friends who are older and younger than me at my part-time job.

9. _____ Many teachers are enthusiastic about teaching their specialties.

10. _____ An important part of university life is being able to make all kinds of friends.

2 Write two paragraphs about both sides of university life. Be sure to start with the topic sentence you chose above.

Academic side of university life

_____

_____

_____

_____

As I have described above, university classes are much more challenging than high school classes.

_____

_____

_____

_____

_____

Thanks to being a university student, I have become friends with many different people.

Simply Writing   _Topic Sentences_

Thinking of a topic sentence is one of the hardest parts of writing a paragraph, but if you have a good topic sentence, writing the rest of the paragraph will be easier. Here are the steps that will help you make a topic sentence.

STEP 1 ▷ Think of a general topic.

Example: college

⬇

STEP 2 ▷ Narrow this idea down into smaller categories.

Example: school life, classes, friends, club activities, teachers, etc.

⬇

STEP 3 ▷ Choose one of the smaller categories and narrow it down again.

Example: classes: favorite class, boring teachers, some are too early in the morning, some are interesting, but hard.

⬇

STEP 4 ▷ Choose one of the smaller categories and think of your opinion about the topic.

Example: classes: interesting but hard

⬇

STEP 5 ▷ Make a topic sentence. Don't forget you need a topic and an opinion / controlling idea.

Example:

Some of my <u>university classes</u> are <u>very interesting, but they are hard.</u>

                topic   _opinion_

Follow these step-by-step directions to make your topic sentence.

STEP 1 ▷ Think of a general topic (**Example:** friendship, education, family, happiness).

_____

⬇

STEP 2 ▷ Narrow this idea down into smaller categories.

_____

⬇

STEP 3 ▷ Choose one of the smaller categories and narrow it down again.

_____

⬇

STEP 4 ▷ Choose one of the smaller categories and think of your opinion about the topic.

_____

⬇

STEP 5 ▷ Make your topic sentence. Don't forget you need a topic and an opinion / controlling idea.

_____

Let's Write

Now that you know how to write a topic sentence, make three topic sentences for each of these topics by changing the opinion.

1. Pets

_____
_____
_____

2. Movies

_____
_____
_____

3. Homework

_____
_____
_____

4. Careers

_____

_____

_____

5. Money

_____

_____

_____

✔ Writing Checklist

☐ Is your name clearly written on the paper?

☐ Is your paper neatly handwritten or typed?

☐ Are all of the necessary words capitalized?

☐ Are all of the words spelled correctly?

☐ Did you use periods, commas, and other punctuation marks appropriately?

☐ Did you use the right verb tense for each sentence?

☐ Are all of your sentences complete sentences with a subject and a verb?

☐ Does your paragraph have a clear topic sentence?

☐ Does your topic sentence have a topic and an opinion?

Chapter 11

WHAT'S A PARAGRAPH? 2
Supporting Sentences and Concluding Sentence

Supporting Sentences

Now that you have your topic sentence, you need to think about the rest of the sentences for your paragraph. They need to follow the topic sentence, and they are called **supporting sentences**. Here are the steps that you can use to write supporting sentences for your paragraph.

STEP 1 ▷ Write down your topic sentence.

Example:
Joining the university soccer team was the best decision I ever made.

⬇

STEP 2 ▷ Make a list of ideas that you want to include in the paragraph. They don't need to be complete sentences.

Example: make friends, have parties, a lot of work, travel together, improve my soccer skills, have the same classes as members of the soccer team, won't have much time for soccer next year because of job hunting, developed leadership skills, etc.

⬇

STEP 3 ▷ Look at the ideas you have written. Choose three ideas that support the topic sentence.

Example: make friends, travel together, developed leadership skills

⬇

STEP 4 ▷ Make sentences out of your ideas.

Example:
I made a lot of friends because I was on the university soccer team.
I learned a lot about leadership after I became co-captain of the team.

Try It Out 1

According to the steps you learned on the previous page, follow these step-by-step directions to write good supporting sentences for your paragraph.

STEP 1 Choose one of the topic sentences you made in Chapter 10 and write it down.

_____

↓

STEP 2 Make a list of ideas that you want to include in the paragraph. They don't need to be complete sentences.

```



```

↓

STEP 3 Look at the ideas you have written. Make sure that they support the topic sentence. Get rid of those that don't support the topic sentence.

```



```

↓

STEP 4 Make sentences out of your ideas.

_____

_____

_____

_____

_____

Simply Writing *Supporting Details*

To make your paragraphs interesting, you will need to give details. If your paragraph has no details, the reader will find it very boring. These details help explain the supporting sentences and they help the reader understand what you want to say. Here are the steps you can take to make your paragraph more interesting.

STEP 1 Write down the sentences that support the topic sentence.

Topic sentence

Joining the university soccer team was the best decision I ever made.

Supporting Sentences

I made a lot of friends because I was on the university soccer team.

I learned a lot about leadership after I became co-captain of the team.

STEP 2 Then write down at least two details for each supporting sentence.

Example:

I made a lot of friends because I was on the university soccer team.

    a. from other departments, other countries, and other schools

    b. have parties, travel together

I learned a lot about leadership after I became co-captain of the team.

    a. not easy to make decisions

    b. people count on me

STEP 3 Write complete sentences from the supporting details.

Example:

I made a lot of friends because I was on the university soccer team.

    a. I've made friends with students from other departments such as math and economics.

    b. There are some exchange students on the team, so I became friends with people from other countries.

    c. We often have parties after tournaments, whether we win or lose.

    d. During vacations, we sometimes take trips together to places like Karuizawa or Nikko.

I learned a lot about leadership after I became co-captain of the team.

    a. I sometimes have to make difficult decisions.

    b. I learned it isn't possible to make everyone happy all of the time.

    c. I learned how to discuss important issues concerning the team in a calm manner.

Concluding Sentence

The last sentence in a paragraph is important because it provides an ending for the reader. It is **the concluding sentence**. Here are some tips on how to write your last sentence.

STEP 1 ▶ Look at your topic sentence.

Joining the university soccer team was the best decision I ever made.

↓

STEP 2 ▶ Rewrite the topic sentence so that it states the same idea in different words.

"My soccer club is one of the best parts of university life for me."

or "My university life is really fun because of my soccer club."

or "If I didn't have my soccer club, I don't think I would enjoy university life so much."

Try It Out 2

Write down the sentences that support the topic sentence and write sentences that explain or support the sentence.

Your topic sentence from Chapter 10

_____

Supporting sentence

_____

a. _____

b. _____

c. _____

Supporting sentence

_____

a. _____

b. _____

c. _____

Supporting sentence

a. _____

b. _____

c. _____

Your concluding sentence

_____

Simply Writing *Concluding Sentence*

There are two ways a writer can conclude a paragraph. First, the writer can remind the reader of the main point by rewriting the topic sentence so that the words are different but the meaning is the same. Second, a writer can summarize the main points of the whole paragraph. Writers also give the reader a hint that the paragraph is ending by adding transition words like "in sum" or "in conclusion."

1 Read the following and match the concluding sentences with topic sentences.

Topic sentences	Concluding sentences
1. Working while studying is a good way for students to learn about society.	a. In conclusion, just cutting back on these small daily expenses can result in having enough money to take the trip of a lifetime.
2. Successful students usually do the following three things.	b. In conclusion, anyone can do their part to help the environment if they change a few small habits.
3. Spending too much time on video games can harm a student's grades.	c. In conclusion, starting your own business is challenging, but there are a few things a person can do to make things go a bit more smoothly.
4. There are several ways students can save money to take a trip.	d. In sum, students can prepare themselves for the real world if they have a part-time job.
5. There are three reasons why I hate horror movies.	e. In sum, some people begin to smoke even though they are aware that it is harmful to their health.
6. A person doesn't have to spend a lot of money to be fashionable.	
7. Packing a suitcase for a week-long trip is easy if you do the following.	

8. A person who wants to become an entrepreneur should take the following steps.

9. Ordinary people can do the following if they want to help save the environment.

10. People start smoking for various reasons.

f. In conclusion, if you choose your clothes carefully and eliminate unnecessary items, you can travel easily for a week with just one small suitcase.

g. In sum, fashion is all about making a statement about yourself and not how much money you spend.

h. In conclusion, these three things can help students have a successful time at college.

i. While some people may love horror movies, I hate them and would never waste my money to see one.

j. Clearly if students spend more time on games than they do on studying, their grades will suffer.

2 Write a concluding sentence that matches each of the following topic sentences.

1. Spending too much time playing video games can harm a student's grades.

_____

2. Everyone should go abroad at least once in their life.

_____

3. I took a memorable trip with my high school friends last spring.

_____

4. Working part-time at a restaurant is challenging, but I have learned many things.

_____

5. Getting a driver's license in Japan involves a number of steps.

_____

Let's Write

1 Choose two of the topic sentences on the previous page and write them down. Then make a memo of what you could say about those topics that follows the opinion / controlling idea.

TOPIC ONE

Topic sentence _____

★ _____
★ _____
★ _____
★ _____
★ _____

TOPIC TWO

Topic sentence _____

★ _____
★ _____
★ _____
★ _____
★ _____

2 Using your notes from above, write two paragraphs. Don't forget to include the topic sentence and the concluding sentence.

TOPIC ONE

_____
_____
_____
_____
_____

TOPIC TWO

_____
_____
_____
_____
_____

✔ Writing Checklist

- ☐ Is your name clearly written on the paper?
- ☐ Is your paper neatly handwritten or typed?
- ☐ Are all of the necessary words capitalized?
- ☐ Are all of the words spelled correctly?
- ☐ Did you use periods, commas, and other punctuation marks appropriately?
- ☐ Did you use the right verb tense for each sentence?
- ☐ Are all of your sentences complete sentences with a subject and a verb?
- ☐ Does your paragraph have a clear topic sentence?
- ☐ Does your topic sentence have a topic and an opinion?
- ☐ Do all of the sentences in the paragraph relate to the topic sentence?
- ☐ Does your paragraph have enough supporting details to make it interesting for the reader?
- ☐ Does your paragraph have a concluding sentence?

Chapter 12

PERSUASIVE PARAGRAPHS
Supporting Opinions

Persuasive Paragraphs

What is persuasive writing? When you write a persuasive paragraph, you are offering your opinion on a topic. Persuasive writing has two purposes. One is to try to convince readers that they should think as you do. Another is to explain to a reader why you think as you do. A good persuasive paragraph has a solid topic sentence and at least five sentences that support the topic sentence and give interesting details.

Try It Out 1

The following sentences are on the controversial topic of animal testing. Decide which ones are for (F) animal testing and which ones are against (A) animal testing.

1. _____ It is cruel to use animals to determine whether cosmetics or household cleaners are safe for humans.

2. _____ Many animal experiments are unnecessary and expensive.

3. _____ Experimenting on animals violates their rights.

4. _____ Since animals have a short lifespan, they can be studied for several generations, and this can help scientists understand how a disease develops and discover how to cure it.

5. _____ Animals used in experiments are often treated badly.

6. _____ Many animals have the same diseases as humans, such as cancer, heart disease, and diabetes.

7. _____ It is not right to make animals suffer so humans can gain knowledge.

8. _____ Because of animal testing, vaccinations and cures for diseases have been discovered.

9. _____ Thanks to animal testing, humans can live longer by having heart and lung transplants.

10. _____ Animals are different from humans; therefore, to get the most information from experiments, humans should be used as test subjects.

1. Make a topic sentence that is for animal testing.

   _____

2. Complete your paragraph by adding sentences that support your topic sentence. Add transition words to make your paragraph smooth. Don't forget to write a concluding sentence.

   _____
   _____
   _____
   _____
   _____
   _____
   _____
   _____
   _____
   _____

3. Make a topic sentence that is against animal testing.

   _____

4. Complete your paragraph by adding sentences that support your topic sentence. Add transition words to make your paragraph smooth. Don't forget to write a concluding sentence.

   _____
   _____
   _____
   _____
   _____
   _____
   _____
   _____
   _____

Try It Out 3

1 Read the following topic sentences and write a list of supporting details for each one.

Topic sentence High school students should not be forced to wear uniforms to school.

- _____
- _____
- _____
- _____
- _____

Topic sentence High school students should wear uniforms to school.

- _____
- _____
- _____
- _____
- _____

2 Write two paragraphs, one "for" and one "against" high school uniforms. Be sure to add the topic sentence, supporting details, and transition words to make your paragraph smooth. Don't forget to write a concluding sentence.

Paragraph A

_____
_____
_____
_____
_____
_____
_____
_____
_____
_____
_____

Paragraph B

_____

_____

_____

_____

_____

_____

_____

_____

_____

_____

Simply Writing | *Supporting Opinions #1: Reasons*

There are three main ways to support your opinion: **reasons**, **examples**, and **voices of experts**.

One way to support your opinion is to give a reason. Reasons are often given with "because" and "since". Look at the following.

Examples:

I believe workers' salaries should be higher **because** the cost of living has increased.

Older people should keep up with modern technology **since** it will enable them to connect with others and access information easily.

Match the opinions below with the best reasons that follow.

1. _____ Elementary school children should not be given cell phones

2. _____ The death penalty should be abolished

3. _____ High school students need to learn how to type on a keyboard before they enter university

4. _____ Paper textbooks should be replaced by electronic books

5. _____ The media should not follow celebrities around

6. _____ High schools should introduce a second foreign language into the curriculum

7. _____ Taking a gap year between high school and university can be advantageous for some students

8. _____ City Hall should not be torn down and replaced with a new building

9. _____ Gas cars and motorcycles need to be replaced with electric vehicles

10. _____ Companies should make sure that 50% of their new recruits are women

a. because they can learn a lot in that year, and they'll enter university with a more mature mind.

b. because it's often given to poor people who cannot afford good lawyers.

c. because it's a beautiful historical structure.

d. since they're easier for students to carry to school.

e. since women represent half of our society.

f. because having this skill will enable them to complete their assignments quickly and in a professional manner.

g. because they're much better for the environment.

h. since speaking multiple languages will be an advantage for workers in the future.

i. because they're entitled to privacy.

j. since they're not old enough to be responsible for one.

Another way to support your opinion is to give an example. Examples are often sentences that follow the reason and they often begin with "for example" or "for instance". Look at the following.

Examples:

I believe workers' salaries should be higher because the cost of living has increased. **For example**, I used to be able to buy a week's worth of groceries for ¥5,000, but now I have to spend ¥7,000.

Older people should keep up with modern technology since it will enable them to connect with others and access information easily. **For instance**, my ninety-year-old grandfather chats online with his friends in different parts of Japan every day.

Match the opinions below with the best examples that follow.

1. _____ Elementary school children should not be given cell phones.

2. _____ The death penalty should be abolished.

3. _____ High school students need to learn how to type on a keyboard before they enter university.

4. _____ Paper textbooks should be replaced by electronic books.

5. _____ The media should not follow celebrities around.

6. _____ High schools should introduce a second foreign language into the curriculum.

7. _____ Taking a gap year between high school and university can be advantageous for some students.

8. _____ City Hall should not be torn down and replaced with a new building.

9. _____ Gas cars and motorcycles need to be replaced with electric vehicles.

10. _____ Companies should make sure that 50% of their new recruits are women.

a. For example, the newspaper recently reported that a man was found innocent five years after his execution.

b. When it was first built it received many architectural awards and people came from far and wide to see it.

c. My older sister works for a company that only hired 30% women the year she was hired.

d. My cousin, for example, spent a year in Australia where he improved his English skills to such an extent he could skip basic English classes at university.

e. I have three or four classes every day, and I have to bring a heavy book for each one.

f. My neighbor's child, for instance, lost his phone at the park only a week after he got it.

g. My older brother now drives an electric motorbike, and he saves several thousand yen a week in gas costs.

h. Their private time, such as when they take their children to school or have dinner with their families, should be protected.

i. It takes me a long time to do my assignments, but my friend, on the other hand, can complete hers quickly because she already knows how to type.

j. Other languages, for example, Spanish and Chinese, are also spoken by many people in the world.

Simply Writing   *Supporting Opinions #3: Voices of Experts*

Writers often use the voice of an expert to support an opinion or a claim. Sometimes a writer will use the expert's exact words. In this case, quotation marks (" ") are needed. Sometimes a writer will summarize the expert's words. Look at the following.

Examples:
In a recent press conference, the Prime Minister **said**, "This is a serious problem that must be solved as quickly as possible, or people will begin to suffer."

One computer manufacturer **said that** they plan to target older customers and make many new devices that will make their lives easier.

Read the following sentences that introduce some experts' words. Then decide if the sentence includes a direct quote (the exact words of the expert) or a summary of the expert's words. Write "D" for direct quote and "S" for summary.

1. _____ According to Dr. Wells, Head of Cardiology at Genki Hospital, "The increase of lung cancer in men and women in their forties is directly related to cigarettes."

2. _____ Professor Ueno, a researcher at Kashikoi University, believes that students today are not as well-equipped for college academics as those of fifteen years ago.

3. _____ One of the greatest soccer players of the 21st century, Andrés Iniesta, has argued that one way out of the ghetto for many poor youngsters is through sports.

4. _____ Rama Burman, the famous chef, says, "The secret to good Indian cooking is being sure to use the freshest spices."

5. _____ When asked about child discipline, Miki Matsumoto, mother of six, said that mothers should teach their children the difference between right and wrong.

Let's Write

1 Write a topic sentence that expresses your opinion for each one of these topics.

a. education _____

b. crime _____

c. fashion _____

d. computers _____

e. travel _____

2 Choose one of the topic sentences above and write a paragraph. Include the words of at least one person to help you support your opinion and be sure to follow the step-by-step paragraph writing techniques you have learned so far.

☑ Writing Checklist

☐ Is your name clearly written on the paper?

☐ Is your paper neatly handwritten or typed?

☐ Are all of the necessary words capitalized?

☐ Are all of the words spelled correctly?

☐ Did you use periods, commas, and other punctuation marks appropriately?

☐ Did you use the right verb tense for each sentence?

☐ Are all of your sentences complete sentences with a subject and a verb?

☐ Does your paragraph have a clear topic sentence?

☐ Does your topic sentence have a topic and an opinion?

☐ Do all of the sentences in the paragraph relate to the topic sentence?

☐ Does your paragraph have enough supporting details to make it interesting for the reader?

☐ Does your paragraph have a concluding sentence?

Chapter 13

THE FIVE-PARAGRAPH ESSAY [1]
Thesis Statement

The Five-Paragraph Essay

Now that you know how to write paragraphs, the next step is the five-paragraph essay. The five-paragraph essay is the backbone of academic writing, but it is not difficult. It is structured very much like an extended paragraph. Look at this outline.

Paragraph 1 Introduction — Introduction to topic, background information, and thesis statement*.

Paragraph 2 Body — Topic sentence related to thesis statement. Supporting sentences and examples.

Paragraph 3 Body — Topic sentence related to thesis statement. Supporting sentences and examples.

Paragraph 4 Body — Topic sentence related to thesis statement. Supporting sentences and examples.

Paragraph 5 Conclusion — Reworded thesis statement or summary of the body paragraphs and final thoughts on the topic.

The first paragraph is the **introduction** which has the thesis statement. The next three paragraphs make up the **body**. Each has topic sentences that support the thesis statement followed by examples and support. The last paragraph is the **conclusion** that often has the reworded thesis statement.

*The thesis statement is the "Queen of the Topic Sentences." She is the boss of your essay and she controls the paragraphs. Like a topic sentence, the thesis statement tells the reader two things: a topic and an opinion (or "controlling idea") about the topic. The difference is a topic sentence tells a reader what a **paragraph** will be about, but a thesis statement tells the reader what the entire **essay** will be about.

So far, you have learned that a topic sentence has a "topic" and an "opinion." In addition to opinion, we also sometimes use the word "controlling idea." The purpose of a controlling idea is not to express an opinion but to tell the reader what the paragraph will be about. Look at the following sentences that show a writer's opinion.

Examples:

High school students shouldn't work part-time for several reasons.

Unhealthy snack foods shouldn't be sold to children.

The death penalty is unethical for many reasons.

Now look at the following sentences that don't express an opinion, but introduce what the paragraph will be about.

Examples:

There are three main reasons why World War I started.

Professional athletes are role models for children in various ways.

Japanese anime and manga spread throughout the world for three reasons.

As you can see, both types of paragraphs require explanation and support, but are not necessarily a writer's opinion.

Try It Out 1

Read the following thesis statement and the topic sentences. Circle the topic in the thesis statement and underline the controlling idea. Notice how each topic sentence deals with one part of the controlling idea in the thesis statement.

Thesis statement

The modern Olympics have become a global sporting event that brings together athletes from around the world, promotes international friendship, and showcases athletic excellence.

Topic sentences

a. The modern Olympics are a worldwide event where athletes from different countries come together to compete in various sports and demonstrate their skills.

b. The modern Olympics aim to foster international friendship and understanding by enabling athletes to interact and share cultural experiences.

c. The modern Olympics celebrate athletic excellence by showcasing the best athletes in the world and providing them with an opportunity to compete with other top athletes on a global stage.

Try It Out 2

1 **Read the following thesis statement and underline the three parts of the controlling idea.**

Traveling abroad is not only an exciting way for college students to spend their summer vacation, but they can also improve their English skills, make friends from all over the world, and experience things they never would have been able to if they had stayed at home.

What is the topic for each of the three points?

(1) _____

(2) _____

(3) _____

2 **Now write three topic sentences (with topic and controlling idea) that fit the thesis statement.**

(1) _____

(2) _____

(3) _____

3 **For each of the topic sentences you wrote above, give three examples of specific support you could use in the paragraph. Remember, you can use reasons, examples, and words from experts.**

(1) **a.** _____

    b. _____

    c. _____

(2) **a.** _____

    b. _____

    c. _____

(3) **a.** _____

    b. _____

    c. _____

Try It Out 3

1 Write a thesis statement dealing with the topic of sports. In other words, you need to decide the controlling idea.

_____

_____

_____

2 Write three topic sentences related to the thesis statement you made.

(1) _____

(2) _____

(3) _____

3 For each topic sentence above, write three examples of specific support you could use in the paragraph.

(1) **a.** _____

    b. _____

    c. _____

(2) **a.** _____

    b. _____

    c. _____

(3) **a.** _____

    b. _____

    c. _____

4 Look at your thesis statement and rewrite it using different words.

_____

_____

_____

Try It Out 4

1 Write a thesis statement about university entrance exams.

_____

_____

_____

2 Write three topic sentences related to the thesis statement you made.

(1) _____

(2) _____

(3) _____

3 For each topic sentence above, write three examples of specific support you could use in this paragraph.

(1) **a.** _____

    b. _____

    c. _____

(2) **a.** _____

    b. _____

    c. _____

(3) **a.** _____

    b. _____

    c. _____

4 Look at your thesis statement and rewrite it using different words.

_____

_____

_____

Transition words connect your sentences. They help the reader understand what you are trying to say. You are already familiar with many of these words, but this handy chart can help you when you write. Think of what you want to do, and choose a word in that category. These words often, but not always, require a comma.

To show time order/listing order

first	next	then	furthermore
also	in addition		
after that	finally		

To give a reason

The first reason is that   for these reasons   The most important reason is

To give an example

for example   for instance   such as

To give an opinion

in my opinion   in my view   I believe that

To start a conclusion

in conclusion   in short   to summarize

To give additional information

also   additionally   and   furthermore   in addition

To give opposite information

however   but   in contrast

First, read the following paragraph. Circle the topic sentence and underline the main supporting sentences. Then draw a square around the transition words.

Joining the university soccer team was the best decision I ever made. First, I could make a lot of friends, not only from my department but also from other departments such as math and economics. We often have parties after games, whether we win or lose. Furthermore, we always have an end-of-the-year party at a very nice restaurant. I also got to know some students on other university teams at tournaments. We often exchange messages with each other and sometimes meet on holidays. In addition to making friends, I've also developed some important leadership skills that will be useful for my future. After I was elected co-captain of my team, I learned it's not easy to make decisions that will make everyone happy. I've also learned how to talk to people in many kinds of situations. I believe this skill will help me when I start to work in society. In short, I'm so glad I joined the soccer team when I was a first-year student because otherwise my university life would not have been this wonderful.

Let's Write

1 Choose one of the following topics, narrow it down and write a thesis statement. Then make three topic sentences that support that thesis statement. Finally, write sentences that provide specific support for each topic sentence.

friendship   careers   education   family   health   natural disasters

Thesis statement _____

_____

_____

_____

Topic sentence _____

Specific support _____

Specific support _____

Specific support _____

Topic sentence _____

Specific support _____

Specific support _____

Specific support _____

Topic sentence _____

Specific support _____

Specific support _____

Specific support _____

2 Write three paragraphs on a separate piece of paper that support your thesis statement.

✔ Writing Checklist

- ☐ Is your name clearly written on the paper?
- ☐ Is your paper neatly handwritten or typed?
- ☐ Are all of the necessary words capitalized?
- ☐ Are all of the words spelled correctly?
- ☐ Did you use periods, commas, and other punctuation marks appropriately?
- ☐ Did you use the right verb tense for each sentence?
- ☐ Are all of your sentences complete sentences with a subject and a verb?
- ☐ Does your paragraph have a clear topic sentence?
- ☐ Does your topic sentence have a topic and an opinion / controlling idea?
- ☐ Do all of the sentences in the paragraph relate to the topic sentence?
- ☐ Does your paragraph have enough supporting details to make it interesting for the reader?
- ☐ Did you include transition words in appropriate places?
- ☐ Does your paragraph have a concluding sentence?

Chapter 14

THE FIVE-PARAGRAPH ESSAY **2**

Introductions and Conclusions

was born in poor country...Her right...was seriously
d. This was not a great start in life for her, sh...country
s abled persons suffer great hard ships, such as being hidden
ed by their families○ In fact, the day she was born her father
g ~~chamed~~ shamed by his daughter's deformity – left the family.
Unfortunately○her mother sent her to private school where she
educat...~~she had to live school~~ leave when her mother ~~dead.~~ died
...persons became athletes to follow their dreams an...
...helped some disabled persons to li...

Introductions

In the previous chapter you learned the basic points of the five-paragraph essay. In this chapter, we focus on the introduction and the conclusion.

The purpose of the introduction is to tell the reader what you will be discussing in your essay and make the reader want to read it. The **motivator** is the part of the first paragraph that grabs the reader's attention. It is what makes the reader want to continue reading. There are several kinds of motivators which are useful for writing a five-paragraph essay.

Try It Out **1**

1 **Look at the following motivators and match them with their style in the following introductions.**

1. _____ contrary opinion
2. _____ story or anecdote
3. _____ surprising statement

a. Study hard! Go to cram school! These are the words that you often hear from too many parents who want their children to go to prestigious universities. They believe that the only way to get to college is to spend endless hours studying and memorizing lots of facts. But they're wrong. My own parents never pushed me to study hard, and I never went to cram school. Contrary to what my friends' parents predicted about my future academic success, I was able to enter a good university on my first try. I'm sure I was successful at getting into university because my family encouraged me to develop my mind and body through high school club activities, volunteer activities, and reading many books that interested me.

b. The other day I was taking a walk along a beautiful beach. The sound of the waves crashing and the sun on my skin were very pleasant. Then a disturbing sight ruined my walk. A lot of garbage, including plastic bottles and plastic bags, had washed up on the shore and seagulls were looking for food in that garbage. Seeing so much human waste was a disheartening reminder of the many environmental crises we face. This essay will explore the issue of garbage on beaches, including its causes, the consequences, and the urgent need for action.

c. It's time to stop allowing legal murders. That is what the death penalty is. People are wrongfully executed because the system of deciding who will receive the death penalty and who will not receive the death penalty is not fair. In addition, once criminals are dead, they cannot reflect over the bad things they have done. Criminals need to be punished, but the death penalty is not the way.

2 **Underline the thesis statement in the above introductions. Then choose one of the introductions and write three topic sentences that could develop three paragraphs on that topic.**

Thesis statement _____

_____

_____

_____

Topic sentence _____

Topic sentence _____

Topic sentence _____

Conclusions

The purpose of the conclusion is to remind the reader of the main point of the essay and to let them know that the essay is finished. Without a good conclusion the reader might turn the page looking for more. A conclusion often refers back to the first paragraph and includes a reworded thesis statement.

Try It Out 2

Look at the following conclusions that are related to the paragraphs in "Introductions" and underline the reworded topic sentences.

a. In conclusion, I'm glad that my parents didn't push me as much as my friends' parents pushed them. I'm glad I didn't have to study hard and go to cram school every day. My parents were pretty smart because they knew the best way for me to prepare for college was being active in sports, helping others, and reading things I enjoyed.

b. I hope that someday, in the not too distant future, I'll be able to take a walk on a beautiful clean beach. I'm afraid, however, if we don't take immediate action to reduce the amount of garbage that ends up in the ocean and find ways to clean up what garbage is already in it, we may no longer be able to enjoy such beaches.

c. To sum up, the death penalty is definitely wrong. Mistakes might have been made by the police, or people might be unfairly executed because of their racial or economic backgrounds. Finally, once killers are dead, they can no longer spend time thinking about their terrible crime or how to repay society. Murderers need to be punished, but killing the killer is not the answer.

Try It Out 3

1 **Write an introduction for the following thesis statement using the three different styles: contrary opinion, story or anecdote, and surprising statement.**

Learning a second language is important because it can open up personal and professional opportunities.

a. _____

_____

_____

_____

_____

_____

_____

_____

b. _____

_____

_____

_____

_____

_____

_____

_____

c. _____

_____

_____

_____

_____

_____

_____

_____

2 Choose one of the paragraphs above and write a conclusion that fits the thesis statement. Be sure to reword the thesis statement and refer back to the introduction.

_____

_____

_____

_____

_____

_____

_____

3 Write three topic sentences and specific support that apply to the thesis statement.

Topic sentence _____

Specific support _____

Specific support _____

Specific support _____

Topic sentence _____

Specific support _____

Specific support _____

Specific support _____

Topic sentence _____

Specific support _____

Specific support _____

Specific support _____

Simply Writing *Editing*

An important part of writing is editing. This is when a writer reads their paper again carefully to make sure there are no mistakes. Students who edit their papers usually get higher grades because they have eliminated small mistakes.

1 Read the following essay about the pros and cons of three different employment industries. Find the twelve mistakes in this essay and correct them.

Japanese college students have to make an important decision before they finish college. They need to decide which type of industry they want to work for. This essay explores the pros and cons of three types of jobs that are popular choices among college students?

One idustry many students hope to work for is the entertainment industry. Most people love to be entertained, so they think worked in the entertainment world would be exciting. A person could meet famous actors or singers while working for a television station. however, people who want to be successful on the entertainment industry have to put in long hours and experience a lot of competition.

Another industry worth considering is the food industry. everyone needs to travel, so jobs in this field tend to be stable. There are many jobs in this industry. They range from manufacturing food to selling food in supermarkets and restaurants,. Like the entertainment industry, the food industry often requires long hours, making it difficult to have a good work-life balance. It is also sometimes difficult to deal about customers.

Many students aim for employment in the IT industry. The work is challenging, and there could be opportunities for advancement. Many IT jobs have a high slarary. One negative point of this industry is the rapid rate of technological development. It may be difficult to keep up with trends when newer and worse technology is invented.

In sum, students should considered carefully when choosing a potential career. Every industry has positive and negative points, and it is important to be aware of them.

⚠ Factual errors

1. _____ ➡ _____

2. _____ ➡ _____

⚠ Verb errors

3. _____ ➡ _____

4. _____ ➡ _____

⚠ Punctuation errors

5. _____ ➡ _____

6. _____ ➡ _____

⚠ Spelling errors

7. _____ ➡ _____

8. _____ ➡ _____

⚠ Capitalization errors

9. _____ ➡ _____

10. _____ ➡ _____

⚠ Preposition errors

11. _____ ➡ _____

12. _____ ➡ _____

2 On a separate piece of paper, write a five-paragraph essay using the thesis statement found in "Try It Out 3." Proofread your paper carefully and then trade papers with your partner to check for mistakes. Rewrite your paper again if necessary.

Let's Write

1 Choose any topic you like for your final project. You can check Appendix IV (p.127) for some ideas if you like. Outline your essay here:

Thesis statement _____

_____

_____

_____

Topic sentence _____

Specific support _____

Specific support _____

Specific support _____

Topic sentence _____

Specific support _____

Specific support _____

Specific support _____

Topic sentence _____

Specific support _____

Specific support _____

Specific support _____

Reworded thesis statement _____

2 Now, on a separate piece of paper, write the first draft of your essay. Then follow your teacher's directions and submit your essay. Check Appendix II (p.124) to see what your final assignment should look like.

✔ Writing Checklist

- ☐ Is your name clearly written on the paper?
- ☐ Is your paper neatly handwritten or typed?
- ☐ Are all of the necessary words capitalized?
- ☐ Are all of the words spelled correctly?
- ☐ Did you use periods, commas, and other punctuation marks appropriately?
- ☐ Did you use the right verb tense for each sentence?
- ☐ Are all of your sentences complete sentences with a subject and a verb?
- ☐ Does the introduction to your essay start with a contrary opinion, story (or anecdote), or surprising statement?
- ☐ Does your introduction have a thesis statement?
- ☐ Do your paragraphs have topic sentences with a topic and an opinion?
- ☐ Do all of the sentences in the paragraphs relate to the topic sentence?
- ☐ Do your paragraphs have enough supporting details to make it interesting for the reader?
- ☐ Do your paragraphs have concluding sentences?
- ☐ Does your essay have a conclusion?
- ☐ Does your conclusion restate the topic sentence or summarize the main points?

Punctuation

1. End every sentence with a period (.), a question mark (?), or an exclamation mark (!).

2. Use commas
  a) when you separate a series of items
  I like biology, math, history, and English.

  b) when you want to set off any word, phrase or clause that interrupts the flow of the sentence
  The student, sad that he failed his college exam for the third time, went home.

  c) when you begin a sentence with an incomplete sentence (i.e. one that is missing a verb or a subject) and join it with a complete sentence
  Slowly walking home, Kaiji was sure that he had failed the university entrance exam one more time.

  d) when you begin a sentence with words such as **when, although, because, after,** or **whenever**
  Whenever I go to bed after midnight, I oversleep the next morning.
  Although I studied hard for the test, I failed it.

  e) when you combine two complete sentences with **for, and, nor, but, or, yet,** or **so** (You can use the acronym FANBOYS to remember this.)
  He studied as hard as he could, but he was never able to pass the test.

3. Use an apostrophe

  a) to show possession (*Jiro's book, Elsa's brother*). It's preferable to show possession this way rather than the long-winded, *the book of Jiro.*

  b) to show that a word or words have been shortened (*couldn't, won't, let's, I'd*).

Rewrite the following sentences using the correct punctuation.

1. Olivias books are missing

2. Shall we go to Rahuls apartment after school

3. Lets eat either Italian Chinese or French food tonight

4. I cant believe I won free tickets to my favorite singers concert

5. The dog ate its dinner and then it took a nap on the chair

6. All you need to make curry and rice is some meat carrots onions and potatoes

7. Although my sister is living in France I only visited England Spain and Switzerland on my tour

8. Didnt you say that we're having a pop quiz in Ms. Greenes class tomorrow

9. After writing your name at the top of the page you should fill in all of the blank spaces

10. Emilys mother is coming to visit next month but I wont be here because I'm going to my brothers wedding

Capitalization

Certain words in English need to be capitalized. The first word of every sentence, the personal pronoun "I," and all proper nouns (the names of people, countries, cities, rivers, mountains, streets, parks, historical events, languages) are capitalized.

Rewrite the following sentences using the correct punctuation.
1. my sister mary arrived yesterday from los angeles.
2. i wanted to study french, but i decided to study german instead.
3. tom and i are having a great time in new delhi, india.
4. the tallest mountain in japan is mount fuji.
5. our school has thai, korean, and chinese students.

Now read the following paragraph and rewrite it by providing the proper capitalization.

dear aunt jane,

it was great seeing you in tokyo last month. i'm so glad that you had time to come and see me even though you were on a business trip to hong kong. you picked the best time to come to japan for a visit. the cherry blossoms were really beautiful, weren't they? did you enjoy going to shinjuku park with my friends, Natsumi and Rin? i think they're studying english now harder than ever after meeting you because they want to visit you in Australia some day. i hope you had a good flight home. say hello to uncle ron and to mary and jim.

love,
Olivia

What an Assignment Should Look Like

Student Name
Student Number
Assignment's Name

TITLE OF ESSAY

If students want to get good grades on writing assignments, they should take steps to make sure their assignment looks proper. Even if a paragraph or essay is well-written, points might be taken off if it looks sloppy or if it is incorrectly formatted. This essay will describe how to submit a paper that will impress your teacher.

First, make sure your name, student number, and the assignment's name are at the top left-hand side of the paper. The title of your essay is below that, in the center of the page. All the lines in your assignment should be double-spaced. That means there should be a space between each line. You should be able to find line spacing options like this in your word processing program.

Your assignment should also be formatted so that your writing is lined up against the left side of your paper. Here is an example of what the setting might look like in your word processing program.

The first sentence in every new paragraph is always indented. That means that the sentence does not start right at the left-hand margin, but in about three spaces. Do not start a new paragraph for every sentence. (You only start a new paragraph when the topic changes or goes in a different direction.) The margins of your paragraph should be about five centimeters on both sides. If you are handwriting your assignment, make sure you use the right side of the paper. The notebook holes should be on the left, not the right. You should skip every line and make sure your writing is neat and readable.

If you follow these guidelines on what your assignment should look like, your paper will be neat and easy to read. You will still have to be careful with your grammar and content, but you will not lose any points for improper formatting.

Email and Letter Greetings

There are several ways to address someone in an email. Look at the following list, which starts with the most formal style and ends with the most informal style. You should only use an informal style if you are very close to the person you are contacting.

1. Dear Professor Smith,
2. Dear Dr. Smith,
3. Dear Mr./Ms. Smith,
4. Dear Personnel Manager,
5. Dear Mary Smith, / Dear John Smith, (this is if you don't know if they prefer to be called Mr. or Ms.)
6. Dear Mary, / Dear John,
7. Hi Mary, / Hi John, / Hi Grandma,
8. Hey Mary! / Hey John!

The following are examples of sentences you can use in the beginning of a formal email.
1. I hope this email finds you well.
2. I hope you had a nice weekend.
3. I hope you are surviving this terrible hot weather.

Then move into the purpose of a formal email.
1. I'm emailing you because…
2. I'm sending you this mail because I'd like to tell you…
3. I'm writing to ask you…

The following are a few examples of how to end your email.
1. Sincerely,
2. Yours truly,
3. Your student,
4. Thank you for your help.
5. Thank you for your help. I'm looking forward to your reply.
6. Love, (for a close friend or relative)

APPENDIX IV

Writing Topics to Consider

1. If you could change one thing in your life, what would it be?
2. If there's one thing you could change about your family, what would you change and why?
3. When you were a child, what did you want to become when you grew up?
4. If you could be any television character, who would you want to be and why?
5. If you could be any character in a book, who would you want to be and why?
6. What would you do if you suddenly won 1,000,000 yen?
7. What's the most difficult decision you ever had to make?
8. What's your most embarrassing experience?
9. Do you believe in love at first sight? Why or why not?
10. If you could make three wishes, what would you wish for and why?
11. Is a lie always bad? Why or why not?
12. What's the most interesting gift you've ever received?
13. What are the advantages of keeping pets?
14. What are some specific things people can do to help protect the environment?
15. Which do you prefer, going out on the weekends or staying home?
16. Have you ever done anything dangerous? What was it? Would you do it again?
17. Describe a time you've gotten lost. Where was it and what did you do?
18. What's important to consider when one is job hunting?
19. Name two jobs that you'd never want to have and why.
20. Describe three famous people that have inspired others by their achievements.
21. What famous person, alive or dead, would you like to meet and why?
22. Describe how one invention in the past changed the world.
23. If you had a robot that could only do three things, what three things would you like it to do and why?
24. Describe the best teacher you've ever had and what made him/her such a good teacher.
25. Do you think that college entrance exams should be abolished? Why or why not?
26. If you could travel anywhere in the world, where would you go and what would you do there?
27. What five things would you bring with you if you were stranded on an island?
28. If you could travel in a time machine, what era would you visit and why?
29. How different is your college life from your high school life?
30. What's more important in life, talent or luck?

本書には CD（別売）があります

Simply Writing
A Step-by-Step Guide to Good Writing
—New Edition—

2024 年 1 月 20 日　初版第 1 刷発行
2024 年 2 月 20 日　初版第 2 刷発行

著　者　Diane Hawley Nagatomo

発行者　福　岡　正　人

発行所　株式会社 金星堂

（〒 101-0051）東京都千代田区神田神保町 3-21
Tel. (03) 3263-3828（営業部）
(03) 3263-3997（編集部）
Fax (03) 3263-0716
https://www.kinsei-do.co.jp

編集担当　今門貴浩　　　　　　　　　　Printed in Japan
印刷所・製本所／萩原印刷株式会社
ISBN978-4-7647-4206-2　C1082